weeknight gourmet dinners

weeknight gourmet dinners

EXCITING, ELEVATED MEALS MADE EASY

meseidy rivera

FOUNDER OF THE NOSHERY

PAGE STREET

PUBLISHING CO.

PAGE STREET
PUBLISHING CO.

First published in 2020 by
Page Street Publishing Co.
27 Congress Street, Suite 105
Salem, MA 01970
www.pagestreetpublishing.com

Distributed by Macmillan, sales in Canada by The Canadian Manda Group.

24   23   22   21   20   1 2   3 4 5

ISBN-13: 978-1-64567-048-3
ISBN-10: 1-64567-048-1

Library of Congress Control Number: 2019951543

Cover and book design by Kylie Alexander for Page Street Publishing Co.
Photography by Meseidy Rivera

Printed and bound in China

Dedication

To Obed, my best friend and greatest love.
Thank you for all your support and for always bragging about me no matter
how much it makes me squirm.

table of contents

Introduction . . . 9

CARBS À LA GOURMET . . . 13
Goat Cheese–Stuffed Shells with
Honey and Chorizo . . . 14

Instant Pot Risotto à la Carbonara . . . 17

Fontina Cheese Waffles with Cremini Mushroom
Sauce . . . 18

Creamy Polenta with Tomatoes and Baked Eggs . . . 21

White Cheddar Dutch Baby with Arugula
and Watercress Salad . . . 22

Anchovy, Caper and Bread Crumb Pasta . . . 25

Creamy Brown Butter Tortellini . . . 26

Peach and Burrata Farro Salad . . . 29

Japanese Fried Rice . . . 30

Saffron Tortilla Española with Spanish Chorizo . . . 33

Spicy Asian Noodle and Herb Salad . . . 34

CHICKEN SO FLY . . . 37
Sheet Pan Miso Butter–Rubbed Roast Chicken . . . 38

Crispy Za'atar Chicken and Cauliflower . . . 41

Chicken and Pâté Banh Mi . . . 42

Ginger Chicken Meatball Ramen . . . 45

Bloody Mary Pepper Bacon–Wrapped Chicken . . . 46

Instant Pot Piri Piri Chicken Wings . . . 49

Ras el Hanout Chicken with Prune and
Olive Tapenade . . . 50

White Wine–Poached Chicken with Lemon
Butter Sauce . . . 53

Grapefruit and Pink Peppercorn Cream
Chicken Thighs . . . 54

All the Herbs Roast Chicken Breast . . . 57

Orange and Whiskey–Glazed Chicken Thighs with
Roast Cherries . . . 58

MOO, BAA AND OINK . . . 61
Herb Lamb Chops with Roast Eggplant Israeli
Couscous Salad . . . 62

Slow Cooker Mulled Wine Short Ribs . . . 65

Slow Cooker Tamarind Sticky Ribs . . . 68

Herb Pork Chops with Blackberry Sauce . . . 71

Spiced Lamb Meatballs and Harissa-Spiced Yogurt
Dipping Sauce . . . 72

Mole Pork Tacos . . . 75

Instant Pot Braised Lamb with Apricots
and Dates . . . 76

Instant Pot Classic Bolognese . . . 79

Instant Pot Beef Bourguignon . . . 80

Slow Cooker Crispy Five-Spice Pork . . . 83

Skirt Steak with Orange and Shallot Gremolata . . . 84

Perfect Herb and Butter New York Strip . . . 87

The Perfect Charcuterie Board . . . 88

FROM THE SEA . . . 91

Whole Roasted Chimichurri Red Snapper . . . 92

Whipped Ricotta and Sardine Toast . . . 95

Shrimp and Coconut Green Curry . . . 96

Mussels with Orange, Fennel and Black Olives . . . 99

Slow-Roasted Lemon Butter Dill Salmon
and Asparagus . . . 100

Smoked Salmon Tostadas with Chamoy . . . 103

Vadouvan Shrimp with Mango-Herb Salsa . . . 104

Smoked Trout and Rye Panzanella . . . 107

Crab and Chile Mango Lettuce Wraps . . . 108

Guava and Pineapple Shrimp . . . 111

KICKING SIDEKICKS . . . 113

Crispy Roasted Brussels Sprouts with
Jalapeño Honey . . . 114

Roast Sweet Potatoes with Tahini Dressing . . . 117

Roast Carrots with Gochujang Glaze . . . 118

Crispy Rosemary and Beef Tallow Potatoes . . . 121

Mediterranean Tomato Salad with Za'atar
Pita Chips . . . 122

Instant Pot Anchovy Butter Whipped Potatoes . . . 125

Crispy Broccoli with Lemony Yogurt . . . 126

Cannellini Beans and Pancetta . . . 129

Potato Salad with Fresh Herb Vinaigrette . . . 130

Edamame Succotash . . . 133

Charred Zucchini with Pesto . . . 134

White Bean and Asparagus Salad . . . 137

SWEET ENDINGS . . . 139

Cherry and Dark Chocolate Galette . . . 140

Sweet Plantain and Coconut Whipped Cream Crepes
with Dulce de Leche . . . 143

Polenta Budino with Strawberry-Rhubarb
Compote . . . 144

Tahini Bread Pudding with Vanilla Sauce . . . 147

Red Wine–Poached Figs with Whipped
Mascarpone . . . 148

Upside-Down Peach-Ricotta Microwave Cake . . . 151

Brown Butter Apple Tarte Tatin . . . 152

Mexican Hot Chocolate Pots de Crème . . . 155

Blackberry and Peach Ginger Clafoutis . . . 156

Lavender and Meyer Lemon Pound Cake . . . 159

LEVELING UP BY
MAKING AHEAD . . . 161

Instant Pot Roasted Bone Broth . . . 162

Slow Cooker Pork Rillettes (Rustic Pâté) . . . 165

Preserved Lemons . . . 166

Cured Egg Yolks . . . 169

Quick-Pickled Veggies . . . 170

Chimichurri . . . 173

My Favorite Basil Pesto . . . 174

Whole Roasted Garlic . . . 177

Compound Butter: Miso, Anchovy, Herb
and Lemon Dill . . . 178

Clarified Butter, Ghee and Brown Butter . . . 179

Acknowledgments . . . 182

About the Author . . . 185

Index . . . 186

introduction

A Little About Me

"Find a job you enjoy doing, and you will never work a day in your life." Mark Twain knew what he was talking about.

My food blog, The Noshery, was just a simple hobby when I launched it back in 2008. After studying pre-law and learning a little too late that being an attorney wasn't meant for me, I was working unhappily as a legal assistant when my husband encouraged me to take some time and figure out my passion. I discovered that I loved everything about food, and by 2011, I was enrolled at Platt College Culinary Institute. In culinary school, I honed my cooking skills, gained confidence in the kitchen and learned how to run a kitchen efficiently. I integrated all of these skills into my blog and focused on sharing with my readers how they can be a chef in their own kitchen.

After culinary school, I was presented with many fantastic opportunities. I worked as a culinary assistant to award-winning blogger, cookbook author and Food Network star Ree Drummond, The Pioneer Woman, for three years. I also provided television production catering for Food Network's cooking show *The Pioneer Woman* and hot food craft services on the set of *August: Osage County,* starring Meryl Streep and Julia Roberts.

Today, The Noshery is my full-time job. As a food blogger, recipe developer and photographer, I've worked with Albertsons, Pompeian, National Pork Board, Tabasco and DaVinci Wines. The Noshery now has hundreds of recipes that reflect my journey from home cook to chef—pairing unique ingredients together with simple cooking techniques, all in search of the perfect bite.

I am so grateful that, because of the encouragement of my husband, my blog The Noshery and the time I invested in culinary school, my passion for food and teaching about food is now my "job."

A Lot About This Book

If you picked up this book, you love food and you love to get creative in the kitchen. You enjoy experimenting with new and unique flavors, and you don't want to limit a fabulous meal to weekends or holidays. It's Wednesday, and you want dinner to be fabulous.

I know all too well that life is busy, and there have been many evenings where I have turned store-bought rotisserie chicken into spaghetti chicken marinara. And you'd better believe the marinara came from a jar. But like you, there are weeknights when I want more. I want to sit down at our table with a delicious plate of food, a glass of wine and "eat civilized," as my culinary school instructor, Chef Curt Herrmann, would say. That is the goal of this cookbook: to help you add a little fancy to the weeknight dinner table.

In *Weeknight Gourmet Dinners*, a great meal and precious time are not mutually exclusive. You'll learn how to make risotto in your Instant Pot® or other multifunction cooker, how a slow cooker can make the most tender short ribs, that miso will change your chicken game forever and that anchovies are basically the butter of the sea. And, if you really want to level up your gourmet game, I'm going to show you a few make-ahead pantry items, such as Cured Egg Yolks (page 169), Instant Pot Roasted Bone Broth (page 162) and Preserved Lemons (page 166), all of which you will find in the chapter "Leveling Up by Making Ahead" (page 161).

The term *gourmet* typically refers to high-quality or specialty food, usually requiring elaborate and expert preparation, which can sound scary and time consuming. I hope to remove that intimidation by sharing a few tips, tricks, techniques and ingredients so anyone can be a weeknight gourmet. I am going to share with you all the secrets I have learned throughout my culinary career, to help make you a boss in the kitchen.

I put a lot of love into each of the recipes in *Weeknight Gourmet Dinners*, and I hope that you enjoy them as much as we do. Now, throw on your apron and pour yourself a glass of wine; it is cooking time.

How to Have a Weeknight Gourmet Kitchen: Get It Together with Mise en Place

There are three keys to an efficient kitchen where you can whip up a glorious meal any day of the week: a well-stocked pantry, essential tools and mise en place.

Mise en place is a French culinary term meaning "putting in place" or "everything in its place" or, in more current terms, "getting it together." Before you start cooking any recipe, regardless of whether it is simple or complex, everything will go smoother if you "get it together" first. Here are a few simple tips on how to mise en place:

- Read the entire recipe more than once. This includes the introduction and any notes in the recipe. This way, you are not surprised by any details halfway through the recipe.

- Gather the ingredients you need, note what tools are required and prep your cookware. For example, if a sheet pan needs to be lined or the oven needs to be preheated, this is the time to do it.

- Prep your ingredients. This means cleaning, peeling, dicing, chopping, boiling water and whatever else a recipe calls for. Also, when possible, plan ahead and prep ingredients the night before. Such things as marinating, dicing vegetables, picking herbs and making dressings can all be done in advance and stored for use the next day.

- Because ingredients lists are written in the order in which the ingredients are used in a recipe, it is best to prep ingredients in the order listed and then arrange them in that order. This will help keep you on track, assure nothing is missed and make cooking faster.

- When possible, line a large sheet pan with parchment paper or foil and arrange your ingredients in piles on it instead of using bowls. This means fewer dishes—all you need to do is toss the liner once finished.

- Use one large liquid measuring cup for measuring all your liquids. Better to clean one large cup instead of five little cups.

- Give your kitchen a quick cleanup after prep. This way, your kitchen is neat before you start cooking.

- Read the recipe instructions one more time before you start cooking.

- Ready? Cook!

It's Not Hoarding If It's Kitchen Tools

A carpenter can't build a bookcase without the proper tools and the same rule applies to a chef. Not having the right tools will make your time in the kitchen challenging, frustrating and less efficient. If you picked up this book, you likely have a well-stocked kitchen. But it is possible some essential items could be missing. Here is a short list of some specialty tools and small appliances that are used in this book.

- Slow cooker

- Instant Pot or other multifunction cooker

- Food processor

- Hand or stand mixer

- Waffle maker

- Cast-iron skillet

- Fat separator

- Spring-release cookie scoops

- Japanese mandoline

- Microplane

- Rimmed baking sheets

- Ceramic ramekins

- Digital meat thermometer

- Cheesecloth and butcher's twine

carbs à la gourmet

WHO DOESN'T LOVE CARBS? They are the ultimate comfort food.

When most people think of carbs, what comes to mind are rich pasta and crusty bread with a billowy center, and this chapter has plenty of these kinds of dishes for your busy weeknights. My Goat Cheese–Stuffed Shells with Honey and Chorizo (page 14) are a wonderful contrast of creamy, sweet and spicy, and they are also perfect to make ahead and freeze. My Anchovy, Caper and Bread Crumb Pasta (page 25), with its briny saltiness, comes together in less than 30 minutes.

I also have some less conventional carb dishes that will make you weak in the knees, such as the one-skillet wonder Creamy Polenta with Tomatoes and Baked Eggs (page 21)—which is baked until the eggs have set but the yolks are still creamy. It's a thing of beauty.

Breakfast for dinner is a treat and I have been known to enjoy a sweet buttery waffle no matter the hour, but what about crisp and fluffy savory waffles that feel more like a full meal, such as Fontina Cheese Waffles with Cremini Mushroom Sauce (page 18)? The waffle batter, which contains fontina cheese, fresh rosemary and garlic, takes only minutes to whip up and cook. And the easy skillet mushroom sauce is so creamy and delicious, you will want to pour it over everything. Prepare the waffles and sauce in advance for an even quicker weeknight dinner.

One of my absolute favorites is the Saffron Tortilla Española with Spanish Chorizo (page 33). Tortilla Española is a traditional Spanish dish of eggs and potatoes. It is simple, filling and comforting. It's also easy to prepare and reheats beautifully. Every carb deserves love, and this chapter is my ode to all the lovely carbs.

goat cheese–stuffed shells with honey and chorizo

SERVES 6

These shells are stuffed with honey-sweetened goat cheese and baked in a spicy chorizo tomato sauce. Stuffed shells have never been so good. Not to mention, I love a baked pasta dish! It's a full meal in one baking dish that is easy to prepare, and it is a great make-ahead dish. See the note for tips to prepare ahead and freeze.

Prepare the shells: Preheat the oven to 350°F (180°C) and bring a large pot of salted water to a boil.

In the pot, cook the pasta shells until al dente, about 8 minutes. Some of the shells may split; you will need at least 24 whole shells for this dish. Drain the shells and immediately run under cold water. Gently toss the cooked pasta shells with the olive oil to keep them from sticking, then set aside.

While the pasta cooks, prepare the filling: In a food processor, combine the crumbled honey goat cheese and ricotta. Process until smooth and creamy. Spoon the filling into a piping bag or a gallon-sized (4-L) resealable plastic bag, then set aside until ready to use.

Prepare the sauce: Heat a large saucepan over medium-high heat. Combine the olive oil and chorizo in the pan. Cook the chorizo for 5 to 8 minutes, or until cooked through. Lower the heat to medium and add the onion and garlic; sauté until the onion is translucent and the garlic is fragrant, about 3 minutes. Add the crushed tomatoes, tomato paste, paprika and salt and stir until well combined.

Spray a 9 x 13–inch (23 x 33–cm) baking dish with cooking spray, then spoon the sauce into the baking dish. Clip a corner of the plastic bag and pipe about a tablespoon (15 g) of filling into each shell. Place the shells in the tomato sauce and bake for 30 minutes.

Remove from the oven, sprinkle the stuffed shells with the Parmesan and bread crumbs, then drizzle with honey before serving.

Shells
12 oz (340 g) jumbo pasta shells

1 tbsp (15 ml) olive oil

8 oz (225 g) honey goat cheese, or 1 tbsp (15 ml) honey + 8 oz (225 g) goat cheese, crumbled

8 oz (225 g) whole-milk ricotta cheese

Cooking spray, for baking dish

½ cup (50 g) freshly grated Parmesan cheese

¼ cup (30 g) dried bread crumbs

Honey, for drizzling

Sauce
1 tbsp (15 ml) olive oil

1 lb (455 g) ground chorizo

½ small onion, minced

3 cloves garlic, finely minced

1 (28-oz [800-g]) can crushed tomatoes

1 tbsp (15 ml) tomato paste

1½ tsp (scant 4 g) paprika

1 tsp kosher salt

NOTE: This dish can be prepared in advance through the point of assembly in the baking dish. Store, covered with plastic wrap and foil, in the refrigerator overnight. Bake according to the directions. Prep and freeze this recipe unbaked for up to 3 months. Defrost in the refrigerator for 24 hours and bake at 350°F (180°C) for 40 minutes, or until heated through and bubbly.

instant pot risotto à la carbonara

3½ cups (840 ml) chicken stock

8 oz (225 g) diced pancetta

½ small onion, minced

3 cloves garlic, minced

1½ cups (300 g) uncooked Arborio rice (see note)

½ cup (120 ml) white wine

½ cup (50 g) shredded Parmesan cheese, plus more for sprinkling

2 tbsp (28 g) salted butter

4 large egg yolks

Salt

Minced fresh parsley, for garnish

NOTE: Do not replace Arborio rice with long-grain rice as it does not have the starch content of Arborio. The starch that is released by Arborio rice is essential to accomplish the desired creamy consistency of risotto.

SERVES 6 TO 8

Risotto is a classic Italian dish that requires time, patience and a great deal of attention. I absolutely adore it but rarely make it, because I do not have the time to give it the attention the traditional way requires. But with an Instant Pot or other multifunction cooker, you can enjoy the creamiest risotto any night of the week. This risotto is inspired by the rich and creamy pasta favorite, carbonara. If you like creamy, salty and cheesy comfort food, you will love this risotto.

In a medium saucepan over medium-high heat, bring the chicken stock to a simmer.

Set an Instant Pot to sauté and add the diced pancetta. Cook the pancetta, stirring occasionally, until the fat has rendered and it begins to crisp, about 5 minutes. Using a slotted spoon, transfer the pancetta to a paper towel–lined plate.

Add the onion and garlic to the rendered fat and cook for 1 minute, or until fragrant. Add the rice to the pot and stir until well combined, toasting the rice for 2 to 3 minutes.

Add the wine to the pot to deglaze it, scraping up any brown bits in the bottom of the pot. Add the heated chicken stock and stir until well combined. Cook at high pressure for 5 minutes. Once done, quick release the pressure.

Remove the cover and stir in the Parmesan, butter and pancetta until smooth and creamy. Quickly stir in the egg yolks, one at time, and season with salt to taste. Serve immediately, sprinkled with Parmesan and garnished with minced fresh parsley.

fontina cheese waffles with cremini mushroom sauce

SERVES 4

Waffles

5 large eggs, at room temperature

1 cup (240 ml) whole milk, at room temperature

¼ cup (60 ml) heavy cream, at room temperature

¼ cup (55 g) salted butter (½ stick), melted

1 tsp minced fresh rosemary

2 cloves garlic, minced

½ tsp kosher salt

2 cups (250 g) all-purpose flour

½ cup (55 g) shredded fontina cheese

Cooking spray, for waffle iron

Mushroom Sauce

2 tbsp (30 ml) olive oil

½ shallot, minced

2 cloves garlic, minced

8 oz (225 g) cremini mushrooms, sliced

1½ tsp (1 g) minced fresh sage

1 tsp minced fresh rosemary

½ tsp kosher salt

¼ cup (60 ml) white wine

1 cup (240 ml) heavy cream

2 tbsp (28 g) salted butter

¼ cup (28 g) shredded fontina cheese

Minced fresh parsley, for garnish (optional)

I love waffles because all that is needed is a bowl, a whisk and a waffle iron. And the sauce is a simple skillet mushroom sauce that would impress any saucier. The best part is that these waffles can be made ahead, plus the sauce only takes a few minutes to put together. If you like, serve the waffles with the All the Herbs Roast Chicken Breast (page 57), for a new version of chicken and waffles.

Prepare the waffles: Heat a waffle iron according to the manufacturer's instructions and preheat the oven to 200°F (95°C).

In a large bowl, combine the eggs, milk, cream, melted butter, rosemary, garlic and salt and whisk until well blended. Make sure everything is at room temperature, as otherwise the butter will seize and clump. Add the flour and whisk until smooth, then stir in the shredded cheese.

Spray the waffle iron with cooking spray. Pour the batter into the waffle iron and cook, according to the manufacturer's instructions, to your desired doneness. Transfer the waffles to a sheet pan and place in the oven to keep warm.

Prepare the sauce: Place a skillet over medium heat and heat the olive oil, about 1 minute. Add the shallot and garlic and sauté until fragrant, about 1 minute. Add the mushrooms, sage, rosemary and salt and sauté for 2 to 3 minutes, or until the mushrooms have softened. Add the wine and bring to a simmer. Slowly whisk in the cream and simmer for 3 to 4 minutes to let the cream reduce and thicken. Stir in the butter and cheese until smooth and melted.

Serve the waffles topped with the mushroom sauce and garnish with minced fresh parsley, if desired.

NOTE: The waffles can be made ahead. Once cooled, place, separated by parchment paper, in gallon-sized (4-L) resealable plastic bags and freeze. Reheat the waffles directly from frozen in a toaster or microwave for 1 minute.

creamy polenta with tomatoes and baked eggs

Sauce

¼ cup (55 g) salted butter (½ stick)

1 lb (455 g) Campari tomatoes, quartered, or cherry tomatoes, halved

1 medium onion, small diced

3 cloves garlic, pressed

2 tsp (10 ml) white balsamic vinegar

Polenta

1 cup (240 ml) whole milk

3½ cups (840 ml) chicken stock or Instant Pot Roasted Bone Broth (page 162)

2 cloves garlic, pressed

1⅓ cups (9 oz [255 g]) instant polenta

⅓ cup (80 g) mascarpone cheese

½ cup (50 g) freshly grated Parmesan cheese

2 tbsp (28 g) salted butter

To Assemble and Serve

4 large eggs

4 large fresh basil leaves, chopped

Freshly grated Parmesan cheese

SERVES 4

Everything you could desire in comfort food is in this dish. It is creamy, saucy and—bonus—there is minimal cleanup because it is prepared all in one skillet. It starts with a bed of cheesy polenta. The polenta is topped with a rich tomato, onion and butter sauce, and then the eggs.

Preheat the oven to 375°F (190°C).

Prepare the sauce: Heat a 12-inch (30-cm) oven-safe skillet over medium-high heat. Melt the butter in the skillet. Add the tomatoes, onion and garlic. Cook for 15 to 20 minutes, or until the tomatoes have broken down. Stir in the vinegar and let simmer another 2 minutes. Spoon the sauce out of the skillet into a bowl and set aside.

Prepare the polenta: Return the skillet to the heat and add the milk, stock and garlic. Increase the heat, bringing the mixture to a boil, then lower the heat to a simmer. Slowly whisk in the instant polenta and cook until the polenta thickens, about 3 minutes.

Add the mascarpone, Parmesan and butter. Stir the polenta until it's well combined and the cheeses have melted. Spread the polenta evenly in the skillet. Spoon the tomato sauce over the polenta. Using a spoon, shape 4 deep divots in the polenta. Crack an egg into each divot. Bake for 12 to 15 minutes, or until the egg whites have set and the yolks are creamy.

Top with the fresh basil and grated Parmesan.

white cheddar dutch baby with arugula and watercress salad

SERVES 4 TO 6

I love making Dutch baby pancakes because they're made with simple ingredients and come together in a matter of minutes, so they're an ideal meal after a long day at work. Although they're traditionally served sweet and for breakfast, I opted to add a special savory gourmet twist: This Dutch baby is made with white Cheddar cheese and herbs, baked until golden, topped with arugula and watercress salad tossed with bacon vinaigrette and finished with pickled red onion (see note).

Pickled Red Onion
½ cup (120 ml) water

½ cup (120 ml) cider vinegar

1 tbsp (13 g) sugar

1½ tsp (9 g) kosher salt

1 red onion, thinly sliced (see note)

Pancake
3 large eggs

1½ cups (355 ml) whole milk

1½ cups (188 g) all-purpose flour

2 cloves garlic, grated

1 tsp minced fresh rosemary

½ tsp kosher salt

¾ cup (86 g) freshly shredded white Cheddar cheese

2 tbsp (28 g) beef tallow, ghee or salted butter

Salad
4 strips bacon, diced

3 tbsp (45 ml) white wine vinegar

½ shallot, minced

1 clove garlic, grated

1½ tsp (scant 8 ml) Dijon mustard

2 tbsp (30 ml) honey

3 tbsp (45 ml) olive oil

1 cup (22 g) packed arugula

1 cup (36 g) packed watercress

¼ cup (30 g) shredded white Cheddar cheese, for serving

Preheat the oven to 425°F (220°C) and place a cast-iron skillet in the oven.

Prepare the pickled red onion: In a small bowl, combine the water, vinegar, sugar, salt and red onion, making sure that the onion is submerged. Set the onion mixture aside.

Prepare the pancake: In a large bowl, combine the eggs, milk, flour, garlic, rosemary and salt. Whisk until well mixed and smooth, about 1 minute. Then, stir in the freshly shredded cheese until well incorporated. Carefully remove the hot skillet from the oven. Place the tallow in the skillet and swirl around until melted. Pour the batter into the skillet and place it back in the oven. Bake for 20 minutes, or until golden and puffy.

While the Dutch baby bakes, prepare the salad: In a small skillet over medium heat, cook the diced bacon for 4 to 5 minutes, or until the bacon is crisp and the fat has rendered. Reserving 2 tablespoons (30 ml) of bacon drippings, transfer the cooked bacon to a paper towel–lined plate to drain.

In a small bowl, combine the reserved bacon drippings with the vinegar, shallot, garlic, Dijon, honey and olive oil. Whisk until emulsified. Remove the Dutch baby from the oven, toss the salad greens with the dressing and top the pancake with the salad. Sprinkle with the bacon, shredded cheese and ¼ cup (30 g) of pickled red onion.

Serve the Dutch baby sliced, with the salad.

NOTE: See the recipe for Quick-Pickled Veggies (page 170) for how to make and store the pickled red onions in advance.

anchovy, caper and bread crumb pasta

2 cups (100 g) torn sourdough bread (see notes)

2 tbsp (30 ml) melted unsalted butter (see notes)

12 oz (340 g) dried bucatini or linguine pasta

3 tbsp (45 ml) olive oil, divided, plus more if needed

3 cloves garlic, thinly sliced

6 anchovy fillets, finely chopped

1 tsp crushed red pepper flakes

1 tbsp (14 g) salted butter

1 tbsp (6 g) lemon zest

2 tbsp (17 g) capers

¼ cup (25 g) freshly grated Parmesan cheese, plus more for serving (optional)

¼ cup (15 g) chopped fresh parsley

NOTES: The bread crumbs can be made ahead and stored in an airtight container. I recommend putting bread crumbs on all of your pasta.

Replace the anchovies and butter with 2 tablespoons (28 g) of Anchovy Butter (page 178).

SERVES 4 TO 6

A great pasta dish only needs a few simple quality ingredients to be fantastic. This meal comes together in no time, and with each bite, you will be transported to a small Italian café.

If you are pumping your brakes at the thought of anchovies, stop now, because anchovies are wonderful salty goodness. They are the key to creating a creamy and perfectly salty sauce. The pasta is also topped with crunchy buttered bread crumbs for texture.

Preheat the oven to 400°F (200°C). Line a rimmed sheet pan with foil and bring a pot of salted water to a boil.

In a food processor, combine the bread and melted butter. Process until the bread is crumbled and well mixed with the melted butter. Spread the bread crumbs on the prepared sheet pan and bake, stirring at the halfway point, for about 8 minutes, or until the bread crumbs are toasted. Set the bread crumbs aside until ready to use.

Add the pasta to the boiling water and cook for 11 minutes, or until al dente. Reserve 1 cup (240 ml) of pasta water, then drain the pasta of the remaining water. Toss the pasta with 1 tablespoon (15 ml) of the olive oil to keep it from sticking together and set the pasta aside until ready to use.

Heat a 12-inch (30-cm) skillet over medium heat. Heat the remaining 2 tablespoons (30 ml) of olive oil and sauté the garlic until lightly browned, about 2 minutes. Add the anchovies and red pepper flakes to the skillet. Cook the anchovies until dissolved, about 1 minute. Add the tablespoon (14 g) of unmelted butter and whisk until smooth. Add the cooked pasta, lemon zest and capers to the skillet. Toss the pasta until it is well coated, then add ¼ cup (60 ml) of the reserved pasta liquid and the grated Parmesan. Toss the pasta until the cheese is melted and it is evenly coated. If the pasta is dry, you can add more cooking liquid and olive oil, then toss again. Add the parsley, toss one last time and serve. Top with the toasted bread crumbs and garnish with more freshly grated Parmesan, if desired.

creamy brown butter tortellini

20 oz (567 g) cheese tortellini

Cooking spray, for cooked pasta

½ cup (112 g) salted butter (1 stick), sliced (see notes)

½ shallot, minced

5 cloves garlic, peeled and cut in half

8 to 10 fresh sage leaves

2 tbsp (30 ml) white wine

¼ cup (60 ml) heavy cream

Salt

Freshly grated Parmesan cheese, for sprinkling

NOTES:

See the recipe for Brown Butter (page 179) for how to make in advance to save time.

If using brown butter that has been made in advance, melt it in a skillet and quickly sauté the shallot, garlic and herbs until fragrant. Then, continue with the recipe as written.

SERVES 6 TO 8

I am going to make a bold personal statement: Brown butter is the bombest butter in all the land. It is butter with its fat solids browned, giving the butter a fantastic nutty flavor. This brown butter is infused with sage and garlic and then tossed with cheese tortellini. However, you can use any tortellini or ravioli you like. If you are craving a really decadent meal, pair the tortellini with the Slow Cooker Mulled Wine Short Ribs (page 65).

Bring a pot of salted water to a boil. Cook the tortellini according to the package directions. Drain and rinse under cool water. Spray the tortellini with cooking spray and toss until well coated, to keep the pasta from sticking. Set the tortellini aside until ready to use.

In a 12-inch (30-cm) skillet over medium heat, heat the butter, stirring often, until just melted, 2 to 3 minutes.

Add the shallot and garlic to the butter and cook for 3 to 4 minutes. The butter will begin to foam and lightly brown; stir to keep the butter from overbrowning. Add the sage leaves and continue to cook until the leaves are dark green and crisp, about 1 minute.

Add the wine and whisk until well combined; simmer for about 1 minute. Lower the heat and slowly whisk in the cream. Continue to whisk until the cream and butter have emulsified.

Add the tortellini and toss until evenly coated and heated through, about 3 minutes. Season with salt to taste and sprinkle with grated Parmesan.

peach and burrata farro salad

Dressing
1 preserved lemon (see note), minced

2 tbsp (30 ml) white balsamic vinegar

½ cup (120 ml) olive oil

1 tsp Dijon mustard

1 clove garlic, grated

Salad
1½ cups (150 g) uncooked farro

½ tsp kosher salt

2 medium peaches, pitted and sliced

1 cup (22 g) baby arugula

4 Campari tomatoes, quartered, or 1 cup (150 g) halved cherry tomatoes

8 oz (225 g) burrata cheese

Maldon salt flakes (optional)

NOTE: Preserved lemon can be purchased online and in the international foods aisle of many gourmet grocery stores. See the recipe for Preserved Lemons (page 166) to make your own.

SERVES 6 TO 8

Farro is a magnificent ancient grain that is grown throughout the Mediterranean and is full of protein and fiber. I believe it should be a permanent fixture in every pantry. It is great because it cooks quickly and has a wonderfully nutty flavor and chewy texture.

I love this salad because the hearty farro contrasts with sweet peaches and tomatoes. The mixture is tossed in a preserved lemon vinaigrette and finished off with creamy cheese. It's the perfect summer salad on its own or served with the All the Herbs Roast Chicken Breast (page 57).

Prepare the dressing: In a small container with a lid, such as a small Mason jar, combine the preserved lemon, vinegar, olive oil, Dijon and garlic. Secure the lid of the container and shake until emulsified, then set aside.

Prepare the salad: In a large saucepan, combine the farro with 3 cups (710 ml) of water and salt and bring to a boil. Then, lower the heat and simmer, covered, for 15 to 20 minutes, or until the farro reaches your desired tenderness. Drain the farro of any of the remaining liquid and fluff with a fork.

In a large bowl, toss together the farro, peaches, arugula, tomatoes and half of the dressing, then toss again until well combined.

Serve the salad, drizzled with more dressing if desired, top with the burrata and sprinkle with the salt flakes (if using) to finish.

japanese fried rice

3 tbsp (45 ml) vegetable oil

6 cups (1 kg) cold cooked jasmine rice (see note)

4 tsp (20 ml) sesame oil

1 tbsp (15 ml) low-sodium soy sauce

1½ tsp (4 g) grated fresh ginger

2 scallions, sliced, green and white parts separated

¾ cup (8 g) bonito flakes

2 (10" [25-cm]) nori sheets, minced

1 tbsp (15 ml) mirin

Cooking spray, for nonstick skillet

4 large eggs

Salt

In my house, we love rice and it's very common to have some left over in the refrigerator. One of my favorite ways to use this leftover rice is Japanese-inspired fried rice. This fried rice uses bonito flakes and nori, which play on fresh salty flavors of the sea. And the best part is that it takes no time to put together.

Heat a 12-inch (30-cm) skillet over medium-high heat. Heat the vegetable oil in the skillet until hot and shimmering, about 1 minute.

Add the rice and sesame oil to the skillet and quickly toss to coat. Spread out the rice in a single layer and leave it undisturbed for 30 seconds. Add the soy sauce, ginger, white scallion slices, bonito flakes and minced nori. Toss until well combined and cook for another 30 seconds. Stir in the mirin and cook for another 30 seconds. Remove from the heat and stir in the green scallion slices.

Heat a large nonstick skillet over medium heat. Lightly spray the skillet with cooking spray and add the eggs. Sprinkle the eggs with salt and cover. Cook the eggs until the whites have set but the yolks are still creamy, about 4 minutes.

Serve the fried rice topped with the cooked eggs.

NOTE: It is important that the cooked rice be cold to keep it from sticking or clumping. The rice can be cooked up to a week in advance and stored in the refrigerator. In a pinch, you can also use prepared rice pouches without heating.

WHAT'S THAT INGREDIENT? *Nori* is a kind of seaweed sold in sheets; six sheets of seaweed snacks can be substituted for the nori. *Mirin* is a rice wine similar to sake, with lower alcohol content and higher sugar content. Bonito flakes, also known as *katsuobushi*, are flakes of dried fermented skipjack tuna. They are used in Japanese cooking to add a smoky and slightly fishy flavor. All of these items can be purchased in Asian markets, online or in the international foods aisle of some gourmet markets.

saffron tortilla española with spanish chorizo

8 large eggs

12 threads saffron

¼ cup (15 g) fresh flat-leaf parsley leaves, chopped

2 cloves garlic, grated

1 tsp kosher salt

¼ cup (60 ml) heavy cream

4 russet potatoes, halved and thinly sliced

2 tbsp (30 ml) olive oil

1 medium yellow onion, halved and thinly sliced

8 oz (225 g) Spanish cured chorizo, diced

Minced fresh parsley, for garnish

NOTE: To make ahead, slice the cooked tortilla into wedges and place in an airtight container in the refrigerator. Reheat in a microwave, covered with a microwave-safe bowl, at 80 percent power for 2 minutes, or until heated through.

SERVES 6 TO 8

I have been making variations of tortilla Española for years. I love this dish because it's composed of simple pantry ingredients and it keeps well, so it's a great choice for a make-ahead dinner. It provides comfort on a cold day and is light enough for a summer patio dinner. Tortilla Española can be enjoyed warm or cold with a lovely leafy salad.

Set your broiler to high. In a medium bowl, whisk together the eggs, saffron, parsley, garlic, salt and cream. Set the egg mixture aside until ready to use.

In a colander, rinse the sliced potatoes under cold water. Transfer the wet sliced potatoes to a microwave-safe bowl along with ¼ cup (60 ml) of water and cover tightly with plastic wrap. Microwave at 100 percent power for 6 minutes, then stir the potatoes and microwave for another 6 minutes. The cooking time can fluctuate a bit, depending on the strength of your microwave. The potatoes should be tender but hold together. If they are still too firm, continue to microwave in 1-minute increments.

Heat a 10-inch (25-cm) nonstick, oven-safe skillet with a lid (set lid aside) over medium-high heat. Heat the olive oil in the skillet for 1 minute. Add the onion to the skillet and sauté until tender, about 2 minutes. Then, add the chorizo and cook for another 2 minutes.

Drain the potatoes, add the onion mixture to the potatoes, then toss until well combined. Add the egg mixture to the potatoes and quickly stir until well incorporated.

Transfer the potato mixture to the skillet and arrange the potatoes in an even layer. Cook, covered, over medium heat for 15 minutes, periodically using a small spatula to lift the tortilla from the pan to keep it from sticking and allow the uncooked egg to run underneath.

Once the tortilla has mostly set, place the skillet, uncovered, under the broiler for 1 to 2 minutes, or until the top has set and browned. Run a spatula along the edge of the tortilla and carefully invert onto a platter. Garnish with minced fresh parsley and slice into wedges to serve.

spicy asian noodle and herb salad

SERVES 4

Dressing
¼ cup (60 ml) vegetable oil

3 tbsp (45 ml) rice vinegar

Juice of 1 lime

4 tsp (20 ml) Asian fish sauce

2 cloves garlic, grated

1 tsp sesame oil

1 tsp grated fresh ginger

1½ tsp (scant 8 ml) chili oil

1 tsp sugar

Salad
10 oz (280 g) curly noodles

1 cup (16 g) loosely packed fresh cilantro leaves

1 cup (24 g) loosely packed fresh Thai basil leaves

1 cup (30 g) loosely packed fresh mint leaves

1 cup (9 g) loosely packed fresh dill fronds

2 scallions, cut on the bias

½ English cucumber, cut into matchsticks

½ cup (60 g) matchstick-cut carrot

1 cup (104 g) mung bean sprouts

1 red chile, seeded and thinly sliced

Salt

1 lime, cut into wedges

NOTE: If you are not a fan of spice, cut the chili oil in the dressing by half and substitute ½ red bell pepper for the red chile.

If you love fresh, bright flavors, you will flip over these noodles. They are loaded with crisp fresh vegetables and aromatic herbs, such as Thai basil, mint, cilantro and dill. The dressing is light, tangy and has a hint of heat. My favorite part about this recipe is that it requires minimal cooking. Also, the noodles and dressing can be prepared ahead of time, leaving nothing else to do but add the vegetables, herbs and dressing to the noodles.

Prepare the dressing: In a small bowl, whisk together all the dressing ingredients until well combined and emulsified.

Prepare the salad: Cook the noodles according to the package directions, drain and run under cold water. In a large bowl, combine the noodles, cilantro, Thai basil, mint, dill, scallions, cucumber, carrot, bean sprouts and red chile. Toss with half of the dressing until well combined. Add more dressing, if desired, and season with salt to taste.

Serve the noodles with the lime wedges.

chicken so fly

PRETTY MUCH EVERYONE EATS CHICKEN because it's the "safe" protein. And, let me be honest, sometimes chicken can be a little humdrum. But with a bit of creativity and pizzazz, you can have chicken that is flavorful and pretty freaking awesome. It's the perfect protein to use when experimenting with new flavors and ingredients, because it allows them to stand out and it's simple to prepare.

Want to elevate your sheet pan meal game? Try the Sheet Pan Miso Butter–Rubbed Roast Chicken (page 38). This recipe really wows. It is loaded with flavor, and no one will be shrugging and saying, "It taste like chicken." This chicken will make all your taste buds stand up and shout. Besides, I don't know a single person who doesn't love a sheet pan meal on a weeknight.

If you are a lover of hot wings, you will swoon over these sweet and spicy Instant Pot Piri Piri Chicken Wings (page 49). Piri piri sauce is made from a combination of crushed chiles, citrus peel, aromatics, spices and herbs. Make sure you stocked up on napkins before digging in.

In the mood for something more refined? Try the All the Herbs Roast Chicken Breast (page 57), which is seasoned with a blend of rosemary, thyme, sage, dill, parsley and tarragon (similar to herbes de Provence). This dish requires minimal effort; all you need is a sheet pan. It's perfect to serve with a light salad or over a bed of roasted vegetables. Dine outside and you will feel as though you're dining at a French café.

Have you ever had a bite of a really good dish and found yourself dancing in your seat? I know I have. My hope is that these recipes take the humdrum out of chicken and replace it with seat dancing and a lot of *mmmmmms*.

sheet pan miso butter–rubbed roast chicken

6 tbsp (84 g) unsalted butter (¾ stick), at room temperature

⅓ cup (83 g) miso paste

1 (1" [2.5-cm]) piece fresh ginger, peeled and chopped

½ medium white onion

3 cloves garlic

4 chicken quarters

2 small bok choy, quartered, or 4 baby bok choy, halved

6 oz (170 g) sliced shiitake mushrooms

NOTE: Pick the chicken off the bones and chop any leftover vegetables to use in the Spicy Asian Noodle and Herb Salad (page 34) or with the Japanese Fried Rice (page 30).

SERVES 4

This chicken is packed full of slap-the-tabletop flavor. The secret is in the umami of the miso butter. Umami is the coveted fifth flavor category that is best described as savory. The result is a very "meaty"-tasting chicken. The chicken quarters are rubbed with miso butter and roasted on a sheet pan with bok choy and shiitake mushrooms for a complete meal. It's almost hard to believe that a dish this easy can have such complex flavor.

Preheat the oven to 400°F (200°C). Line a rimmed sheet pan with foil and set aside.

In a food processor, combine the butter, miso, ginger, onion and garlic. Process until a paste forms, scraping down the sides as needed.

Arrange the chicken quarters on the prepared sheet pan, being careful not to crowd them. Reserving ¼ cup (55 g) of the butter mixture, gently separate the skin from the chicken and stuff 1 tablespoon (14 g) of the butter mixture under the skin. Rub the outside of the chicken quarters with the remaining unreserved butter mixture. Roast in the oven for 30 minutes.

Remove from the oven and carefully transfer the chicken quarters to a plate. Spread the bok choy and shiitake mushrooms on the sheet pan. Dollop the vegetables with the reserved butter mixture and place the chicken quarters over the bok choy. Return the chicken to the oven and roast for another 10 minutes.

Serve the chicken quarters with the bok choy and mushrooms.

WHAT'S THAT INGREDIENT? Miso paste is a Japanese seasoning made from fermented soybeans that are mixed with salt and *koji*, a rice fungus used to make sake. The paste may also include barley, rice, rye or other grains. It can be found in plastic tubs or jars in the refrigerated section of Asian grocery stores, or next to the refrigerated tofu in large grocery stores and natural food stores. See the recipe for Miso Butter (page 178) for how to make and store your own in advance.

crispy za'atar chicken and cauliflower

2 tbsp (30 ml) melted ghee or clarified butter (see notes)

3 tbsp (23 g) za'atar

1 tbsp (15 ml) fresh lemon juice

1½ tsp (9 g) kosher salt

1 head cauliflower, cut into florets (about 4 cups [400 g])

1 red onion, cut into 1" (2.5-cm) wedges

3 heads garlic, tops trimmed

2 lemons, halved

2 lbs (905 g) bone-in, skin-on chicken thighs (4 large thighs)

NOTES: The chicken can be seasoned the night before and stored in a resealable plastic bag in the refrigerator until ready to cook, to get your dinner on the table even faster.

See the recipe for Clarified Butter, Ghee and Brown Butter (page 179) to make your own.

SERVES 4

Za'atar is a Middle Eastern spice blend of dried herbs, sesame seeds and sumac. It's very savory and aromatic, and I recommend everyone add it to their pantry. These chicken thighs are seasoned with za'atar and roasted with cauliflower, red onion, lemons and whole garlic until the chicken is tender and the skin is crispy. You literally put everything on a sheet pan, rub it with seasonings and toss it in the oven. It is a full Middle Eastern–inspired meal. Enjoy the chicken as prepared or served with basmati rice, warm naan bread or the Roast Sweet Potatoes with Tahini Dressing (page 117).

Preheat the oven to 425°F (220°C) and line a rimmed sheet pan with foil.

In a small bowl, combine the melted ghee, za'atar, lemon juice and salt. Place the cauliflower, onion, garlic heads, halved lemons and chicken on the prepared sheet pan. Add the seasoning mixture and toss until evenly coated. Arrange everything into a single layer on the pan.

Bake for 40 to 45 minutes, then broil on high for 1 minute, or until the skin is crispy. Squeeze the roasted garlic cloves out of the heads and sprinkle over the chicken, then serve.

chicken and pâté banh mi

Pickled Vegetables
½ cup (55 g) shredded carrot

½ cup (60 g) thinly sliced English cucumber

½ cup (80 g) sliced red onion

½ cup (120 ml) rice vinegar

1 tbsp (13 g) sugar

¼ tsp kosher salt

½ cup (120 ml) water

Chicken
1 lb (455 g) boneless, skinless chicken thighs, sliced into ½" (1.3-cm) strips

2 tbsp (30 ml) Asian fish sauce

1 tbsp (15 ml) low-sodium soy sauce

1 tbsp (15 ml) vegetable oil

1 tbsp (15 ml) sesame oil

1 tsp sugar

2 tsp (10 ml) sriracha

4 cloves garlic, minced

1 scallion, white part minced, green part sliced on the bias

Zest of 1 lime

1 tsp fresh lime juice

¼ cup (10 g) chopped fresh Thai basil leaves

To Assemble
4 bolillos or hero rolls

¼ cup (60 g) mayonnaise

7 oz (198 g) pork pâté or rillettes (see notes)

Fresh cilantro leaves, for serving

SERVES 4

I know what you are thinking: A sandwich is gourmet? But this isn't a regular sandwich. Banh mi is the ultimate melding of two cultures, Vietnamese and French, in a sandwich—a hearty sandwich that makes a great weeknight dinner. Banh mi traditionally is a French baguette filled with Vietnamese marinated pork, pickled vegetables and cilantro along with French pâté and mayonnaise. This recipe uses quickly marinated chicken thighs and store-bought pork pâté, for a quick and easy sandwich loaded with flavor.

Prepare the pickled vegetables: In a small bowl, combine the carrot, cucumber and red onion. Add the vinegar, sugar, salt and water and toss until well combined, then set aside.

Prepare the chicken: In a medium bowl, combine the chicken with the fish sauce, soy sauce, vegetable oil, sesame oil, sugar, sriracha, garlic and white parts of the scallion. Toss until the additions are well combined and the chicken is evenly coated.

Heat a large skillet over medium-high heat. Add the chicken to the skillet in a single layer and leave it to sear for 1 to 2 minutes before stirring. Continue to cook, stirring occasionally, until cooked through, 3 to 4 minutes. Add the lime zest and juice and Thai basil to the chicken and toss until well combined. Remove from the heat and set aside.

Assemble the banh mi: Split the rolls lengthwise and spread evenly with the mayonnaise. Thinly slice the pâté and place 4 to 5 slices of pâté in each roll. If using rillettes, spread ¼ cup (54 g) in each roll. Divide the chicken evenly among the rolls and top with cilantro leaves and pickled vegetables.

NOTES:
The chicken can be prepared and left to marinate overnight. You can also double the chicken to make more sandwiches or to serve with the Japanese Fried Rice (page 30) or Spicy Asian Noodle and Herb Salad (page 34).

See the recipe for Slow Cooker Pork Rillettes (Rustic Pâté) (page 165) for how to prepare at home in advance.

ginger chicken meatball ramen

Meatballs
1 lb (455 g) ground chicken

1 large egg

⅓ cup (38 g) plain dried bread crumbs

1 tsp grated fresh ginger

1 scallion, white part minced, green part sliced on the bias

1 tsp kosher salt

1 tsp sesame oil

2 tsp (10 ml) rice vinegar

1 tsp sriracha, plus more for garnish

Ramen
2 large eggs

2 cups (475 ml) water

1 (10" [25-cm]) sheet nori, crumbled

4 cups (946 ml) chicken stock or chicken bone broth (page 162)

1 cup (67 g) sliced shiitake mushrooms

1 cup (10 g) bonito flakes

2 cloves garlic, grated

1 tbsp (15 ml) low-sodium soy sauce

1 tsp grated fresh ginger

6.2 oz (176 g) ramen noodles

2 baby bok choy, quartered

Salt (optional)

WHAT'S THAT INGREDIENT?
Nori is the Japanese name for edible seaweed. Six sheets of seaweed snacks can be substituted for the nori. Both of these items can be found in the international foods aisle of gourmet grocery stores.

SERVES 4

Traditionally, broth for ramen requires hours of cooking to accomplish its complex flavor. However, who wants to spend hours simmering broth on a weeknight? To get the desired flavor of ramen, I added bonito flakes and nori to give it that satisfying umami element. Also, the ginger chicken meatballs cook in the broth, adding to the taste and resulting in tender meatballs.

Prepare the meatballs: In a food processor, combine the ground chicken, egg, bread crumbs, ginger, minced white scallion, salt, sesame oil, vinegar and sriracha. Pulse until the mixture is well combined, scraping down the sides as needed. Set the mixture aside.

Prepare the ramen: To boil the eggs, bring a pot of salted water to a boil. Add the eggs and cook for 7 minutes for medium eggs, or 9 minutes for hard-cooked eggs. Drain the eggs and let cool in a bowl of ice water. Once cooled, peel and slice the egg in half and set aside.

Meanwhile, in a microwave-safe measuring cup, combine the water and nori. Heat in a microwave at 100 percent power for 90 seconds and stir. Strain the nori through a fine-mesh strainer into a large pot with a lid (set lid aside).

Add the chicken stock, mushrooms, bonito flakes, garlic, soy sauce and ginger to the pot and bring to a boil. When the stock is boiling, use a 1½-inch (4-cm) spring-loaded cookie scoop to scoop and drop rounded portions of the chicken mixture into the stock. (Do not stress over the shape of the meatballs.) As you add the chicken meatballs to the stock, it will stop boiling; that is fine. You should end up with 15 to 16 meatballs.

Increase the heat and return the stock to a boil. Once it starts to boil, cover, lower the heat and simmer the meatballs for 4 minutes.

Add the ramen noodles and bok choy and cook for an additional 4 minutes, or until the noodles are done. Taste the broth and season with salt to taste, if needed.

Serve in individual bowls, garnished with sliced green scallion, sriracha and ½ boiled egg.

bloody mary pepper bacon–wrapped chicken

32 oz (946 ml) Bloody Mary mix (I recommend McClure's)

4 (5- to 6-oz [140- to 170-g]) boneless, skinless chicken breasts

2 tbsp (30 ml) tomato paste

1 tsp prepared horseradish

1 tsp white wine vinegar

½ tsp sriracha

1½ tsp (scant 8 g) light brown sugar

8 strips black pepper bacon

NOTE: Although the recipe only calls for a 30-minute marinade, I recommend putting the chicken in to marinate the first thing in the morning or the day before. This way, you infuse the most flavor and are ready to cook as soon as dinnertime comes around. The sauce can also be prepared ahead.

SERVES 4

Over-the-top Bloody Marys that can double as a full meal are the latest trend. These elaborate cocktails, some garnished with sliders and fried chicken, inspired me to create this Bloody Mary bacon-wrapped chicken breast. After a short marinade in Bloody Mary mix, these chicken breasts are infused with all the tangy and peppery flavor of the brunch cocktail. Once marinated, they are wrapped with pepper bacon, brushed with a sauce and roasted in the oven. This isn't your average chicken dinner and it is sure to satisfy even non–Bloody Mary lovers.

Set aside 1 tablespoon (15 ml) of the Bloody Mary mix. Then, combine the chicken breast and remaining Bloody Mary mix in a resealable plastic bag. Refrigerate and let marinate for 30 minutes or up to overnight.

Place one oven rack in the center of the oven and the second rack at the top. Preheat the oven to 375°F (190°C) and line a rimmed sheet pan with foil.

While the chicken marinates, combine the tomato paste, reserved Bloody Mary mix, horseradish, vinegar, sriracha and brown sugar in a small bowl and mix well.

Remove the chicken from the marinade and pat dry with clean paper towels. Wrap each chicken breast with 2 slices of pepper bacon, tucking in the ends. Place the bacon-wrapped breasts on the prepared sheet pan. Spread the tomato mixture evenly on the chicken breasts.

Roast in the oven for 30 minutes, or until the internal temperature of a breast reaches 165°F (73°C). Set the broiler to low, and once the broiler coil is red, transfer the pan to the top rack and broil for 1 to 2 minutes, or until the bacon is nicely browned. Serve warm.

instant pot piri piri chicken wings

Piri Piri Sauce

½ cup (112 g) salted butter (1 stick), melted

1 tbsp (15 ml) olive oil

¼ cup (40 g) diced onion

1½ tsp (scant 8 ml) red wine vinegar

1 to 2 tbsp (15 to 30 ml) Thai chili paste or sriracha, depending on desired heat

3 cloves garlic, grated

4 oz (115 g) pimientos

1 tbsp (15 g) light brown sugar

Juice of ½ lime

¼ cup (4 g) fresh cilantro, plus more for garnish

Cooking spray, for pan

12 chicken wings, tips discarded, cut into drumettes and flats

½ cup (120 ml) water

½ tsp kosher salt

SERVES 6

Step aside, buffalo chicken wings—there are some new wings in town. These are cooked in an Instant Pot or other multifunction cooker until they are fall-off-the-bone tender. They are then quickly broiled in the oven until crispy and tossed in a butter and piri piri–inspired sauce. The wings are crispy, spicy, messy and downright addictive.

If you are a hot sauce lover, you must add piri piri sauce to your collection. With origins in both Africa and Portugal, this sauce gets its name from the piri piri chile that was brought over from Angola and Mozambique by Portuguese settlers.

Prepare the piri piri sauce: In a food processor, combine the butter, olive oil, onion, vinegar, chili paste, garlic, pimientos, brown sugar, lime and cilantro. Process until well mixed and smooth. Transfer the sauce to a saucepan and bring to a simmer over medium-high heat, then cook for 5 minutes.

Set your broiler to high and line a rimmed sheet pan with foil. Place a rack in the sheet pan and spray with cooking spray.

Toss the chicken wings with ¼ cup (60 ml) of piri piri sauce. Place the wings and ½ cup (120 ml) of water in a steamer basket in an Instant Pot. Set to cook for 10 minutes on high pressure.

Once done, quick release the pressure. Transfer the wings to a large bowl and toss with the salt. Then, arrange the wings in a single layer in the prepared sheet pan. Place under the broiler for 3 to 4 minutes per side, or until crisp.

Toss the chicken wings with the remaining sauce and serve garnished with cilantro.

ras el hanout chicken with prune and olive tapenade

Filling

½ cup (50 g) Castelvetrano olives, pitted

10 prunes, pitted

1 preserved lemon (see notes)

3 cloves garlic

2 tbsp (17 g) capers

½ cup (32 g) packed fresh parsley leaves

1 tsp white wine vinegar

¼ cup (60 ml) olive oil

Chicken

4 boneless, skinless chicken breasts

2 tsp (5 g) ras el hanout

½ tsp ground cinnamon

½ tsp paprika

½ tsp granulated garlic

1 tsp kosher salt

3 tbsp (42 g) ghee, divided

NOTES:

The chicken breasts can be stuffed with the filling a day ahead. Store, covered with plastic wrap, on a sheet pan in the refrigerator.

Preserved lemon can be purchased online and at many gourmet grocery stores in the international foods aisle. Or see the Preserved Lemons recipe (page 166) to make your own.

SERVES 4

This dish was inspired by the Silver Palate's Chicken Marbella, a French dish consisting of chicken roasted with white wine, prunes and olives. I thought to give it a Moroccan twist, seasoning chicken breasts with ras el hanout and stuffing them with a mixture of olives, prunes and preserved lemon. Serve the chicken with basmati rice, Roast Sweet Potatoes with Tahini Dressing (page 117) or Crispy Broccoli with Lemony Yogurt (page 126).

Prepare the filling: In a food processor, combine the olives, prunes, preserved lemon, garlic, capers, parsley and vinegar. Pulse to roughly chop, then with the food processor on low speed, slowly add the olive oil through the opening in the lid, continuing to process until a paste forms. Set the filling aside.

Prepare the chicken: Place a chicken breast on a cutting board. Holding the breast firmly, carefully make a slit about 3 inches (7.5 cm) wide into the side, starting at the thickest part of the breast. Using the knife, make a cut that goes three-quarters of the way into the breast to make a pocket. Repeat with the remaining chicken breasts.

In a small bowl, stir together the ras el hanout, cinnamon, paprika, granulated garlic and salt until well mixed, then sprinkle the seasoning mixture evenly on all sides of the chicken breasts.

Using a spoon, stuff the filling into the pocket of each chicken breast. It is okay to overstuff the pockets, as the filling will break down some as it cooks. Heat a large cast-iron or heavy-bottomed stainless-steel skillet over medium-high heat. Melt 2 tablespoons (28 g) of the ghee in the skillet, swirling the pan to evenly distribute the ghee. Carefully add the chicken breasts, top side down, to the skillet and cook for 5 minutes, leaving the chicken alone to crisp before flipping.

Flip the chicken breasts and add the remaining tablespoon (14 g) of ghee to the skillet, carefully swirling the pan to distribute the melted ghee around the breasts. Cook for 5 to 7 minutes, or until the internal temperature of a breast reaches 165°F (73°C). Transfer the chicken breasts to a plate to rest for 5 minutes before serving. Serve with any filling that may have fallen out of the pockets.

white wine–poached chicken with lemon butter sauce

4 (6-oz [170-g]) boneless, skinless chicken breasts

¼ cup (56 g) salted butter (½ stick), divided

1 shallot, minced

1 cup (240 ml) white wine

½ cup (120 ml) chicken stock

2 sprigs thyme

1 sprig rosemary

2 fresh sage leaves

1 bay leaf

3 strips lemon zest

2 tbsp (30 ml) heavy cream

Kosher salt

Lemon wedges, for serving

Minced fresh thyme, rosemary and sage, for serving

SERVES 4

While I was in culinary school, one of our final exams was to prepare a number of dishes using different cooking techniques. One of the dishes required us to poach chicken breast in white wine and make a sauce. This recipe is reminiscent of one of those final dishes. The chicken is gently poached in wine, herbs and lemon zest until tender. Then, the same liquid is reduced to make a rich lemon butter sauce. It is the perfect elegant one-skillet dinner to make on a busy weeknight. Serve with White Bean and Asparagus Salad (page 137) or Potato Salad with Fresh Herb Vinaigrette (page 130).

Place the chicken breasts between 2 sheets of plastic wrap and, using a rolling pin, gently flatten them to an even thickness.

Heat a heavy-bottomed 12-inch (30-cm) skillet with a lid (set lid aside) over medium-high heat. Melt 2 tablespoons (28 g) of the butter in the skillet. Add the shallot and sauté for 1 to 2 minutes.

Add the wine, chicken stock, thyme, rosemary, sage leaves, bay leaf and lemon zest to the skillet. Bring the liquid to a boil, then lower the heat to a simmer.

Carefully add the chicken breasts to the poaching liquid and cover. Simmer for 15 minutes, or until tender. Transfer the chicken to a plate.

Remove the herbs and zest from the poaching liquid. Bring the liquid to a boil and continue to boil, uncovered, until reduced by half, about 5 minutes. Whisk in the remaining 2 tablespoons (28 g) of butter and the cream and let simmer for another 2 minutes to thicken. Season the sauce with salt to taste.

Return the chicken to the skillet to warm and serve with the sauce, garnished with lemon wedges and minced herbs.

grapefruit and pink peppercorn cream chicken thighs

Chicken
2 lbs (905 g) bone-in, skin-on chicken thighs (4 large thighs)

1 tsp grapefruit zest

¼ tsp crushed pink peppercorns

1 clove garlic, grated

1 tsp kosher salt

¼ tsp minced fresh rosemary

2 tbsp (30 ml) grapefruit juice

2 tbsp (30 ml) olive oil, divided

Sauce
½ shallot, minced

1 tsp minced fresh rosemary

¼ cup (60 ml) grapefruit juice

1 tbsp (15 ml) white wine

1½ tsp (scant 3 g) crushed pink peppercorns

½ cup (120 ml) heavy cream

1 tbsp (14 g) salted butter

¼ cup (58 g) grapefruit segments, for garnish

Minced fresh parsley or rosemary, for garnish

NOTES:
The chicken thighs can be seasoned ahead and stored in a resealable plastic bag in the refrigerator. This will save time and allow the flavor of the chicken thighs to further develop.

To save time, you can purchase no-sugar-added grapefruit segments in the fruit section of the grocery store.

SERVES 4

I am kind of obsessed with grapefruit—I absolutely love its bright sweet and tart flavor. Here, it pairs perfectly with the delicate taste of pink peppercorns. Even if you don't consider yourself a fan of grapefruit, you will swoon over this 30-minute meal. The chicken is cooked until the skin is crisp and is served with a light and creamy sauce. These creamy chicken thighs can be served with Crispy Rosemary and Beef Tallow Potatoes (page 121) or al dente pasta noodles.

Preheat the oven to 450°F (230°C).

Prepare the chicken: In a large bowl, combine the chicken thighs, grapefruit zest, crushed pink peppercorns, garlic, salt, rosemary, grapefruit juice and 1 tablespoon (15 ml) olive oil. Toss until the seasonings are well combined and the chicken is evenly coated with seasoning.

Heat 1 tablespoon (15 ml) of the olive oil in a 12-inch (30-cm) oven-safe skillet over medium-high heat. Once the oil is shimmering, about 1 minute, sear the chicken thighs, skin side down, for 3 minutes, or until the thighs no longer stick to the skillet. Turn and sear for another 2 to 3 minutes.

Transfer the skillet to the oven and roast for 20 minutes, or until the internal temperature of the thighs reaches 165°F (73°C). While the chicken is in the oven, line a rimmed sheet pan with foil.

Remove the skillet from the oven and transfer the chicken thighs to the prepared sheet pan. Tent with foil and set aside.

Prepare the sauce: Pour out any drippings in the skillet, then reheat the skillet over medium heat. Add the minced shallot and rosemary and sauté until fragrant, about 1 minute. Add the grapefruit juice and wine to deglaze the pan, scraping up all the brown bits in the bottom of the skillet.

Add the crushed pink peppercorns and cream to the skillet and whisk until well combined. Bring to a simmer and let reduce for 5 minutes to thicken. Add the butter and whisk until velvety and emulsified.

Return the chicken thighs to the skillet to warm for 5 minutes. Serve the thighs with the sauce, garnished with grapefruit segments and minced parsley or rosemary.

all the herbs roast chicken breast

Cooking spray, for pan

4 bone-in, skin-on chicken breasts

1 tbsp (4 g) minced fresh parsley

1 tbsp (scant 3 g) minced fresh sage

1 tbsp (4 g) chopped fresh dill

1 tbsp (2 g) chopped fresh thyme

1 tbsp (scant 5 g) chopped fresh tarragon

1 tbsp (2 g) minced fresh rosemary

1 tsp kosher salt, plus more for sprinkling

½ cup (112 g) salted butter (1 stick), at room temperature

1 tsp lemon zest

1 tbsp (15 ml) olive oil

Freshly ground black pepper

NOTE: To save time, rub the chicken breasts with the herb butter ahead of time and place on a foil-lined sheet pan. Cover tightly with plastic wrap and store overnight in the refrigerator.

SERVES 4

This chicken is a staple at my house! I will often cook extra breasts to use during the week to add to salads or pasta for an effortless lunch or dinner. It's also fantastic in chicken salad. I named it All the Herbs Roast Chicken Breast because it uses virtually all the fresh herbs. It is vital to use bone-in, skin-on chicken breast to achieve a tender, juicy breast.

Preheat the oven to 450°F (230°C). Line a rimmed sheet pan with foil and spray with cooking spray.

Place the chicken breasts on the prepared sheet pan. Gently separate the skin from the chicken, creating a pocket under the skin. Be careful not to tear or completely separate the skin from the chicken breast.

In a small bowl, combine the parsley, sage, dill, thyme, tarragon, rosemary, salt, butter and lemon zest. Stir everything together until well mixed.

Spoon 2 tablespoons (28 g) of the butter mixture under the skin of each chicken breast. Press down on the skin and spread out the butter under the skin. It's okay if some of it squeezes out the sides.

Drizzle the chicken breasts with olive oil and sprinkle with salt and pepper. Roast the chicken breasts in the oven for 25 minutes. Rotate the sheet pan and tent the chicken with foil. Lower the oven temperature to 425°F (220°C) and roast for another 25 minutes, or until the internal temperature of a chicken breast reaches 165°F (73°C). Remove the chicken breasts from the oven and set aside to rest for 10 minutes before serving.

orange and whiskey–glazed chicken thighs with roast cherries

SERVES 4 TO 6

Glaze

¼ cup (60 ml) fresh orange juice

1 clove garlic, grated

1 tbsp (15 g) light brown sugar

2 tbsp (30 ml) whiskey

3 tbsp (60 g) orange marmalade

3 dashes of Angostura bitters

Chicken

Zest of 1 orange

1 tbsp (15 ml) fresh orange juice

½ tsp ground nutmeg

3 cloves garlic

2 tbsp (30 ml) olive oil

1 tbsp (18 g) kosher salt

4 lbs (1.8 kg) chicken thighs (about 6 thighs), excess skin trimmed

1½ cups (455 g) frozen dark cherries (about 1 lb)

1 cup (455 g) frozen pearl onions (about 1 lb)

NOTES:

The chicken can be seasoned ahead, stored in a resealable plastic bag and refrigerated overnight. The glaze can also be made a day in advance.

If you do not have a 15 x 21–inch (38 x 53–cm) rimmed sheet pan, you can use two 13 x 18–inch (33 x 45–cm) rimmed sheet pans. Just make sure to rotate the racks halfway during roasting, for even cooking.

I have a deep love for all cocktails made with bourbon or whiskey. This dish was inspired by the classic Manhattan. The chicken thighs are tossed with orange zest and spices and roasted on a sheet pan with dark cherries. They are then finished with an orange and whiskey glaze that is seasoned with a few dashes of Angostura bitters, because you can't have a proper Manhattan without bitters. Chicken thighs can be paired with Instant Pot Anchovy Butter Whipped Potatoes (page 125) or Crispy Roasted Brussels Sprouts with Jalapeño Honey (page 114).

Preheat the oven to 450°F (230°C) and line a 15 x 21–inch (38 x 53–cm) rimmed sheet pan with foil. It is important not to crowd the chicken, to allow the skin to crisp.

Prepare the glaze: In a medium saucepan, whisk together the orange juice, garlic, brown sugar, whiskey and orange marmalade until well combined. Over medium-high heat, bring to a slow boil, then lower the heat to a simmer and continue to cook, whisking, for 5 minutes. Remove from the heat and add the bitters, then whisk again until incorporated.

Prepare the chicken: In a small bowl, combine the orange zest, orange juice, nutmeg, garlic, olive oil and salt and mix well.

Spread the chicken thighs, cherries and pearl onions on the prepared sheet pan. Drizzle with the orange zest mixture and mix everything together until well coated with the seasoning. Arrange the chicken thighs skin side up, leaving a good amount of space between them.

Brush the chicken thighs with half of the orange glaze and roast in the oven for 30 minutes. Then, glaze the thighs with the remaining glaze and roast for another 15 minutes, or until the glaze is sticky and the chicken reaches an internal temperature of 165°F (73°C).

Serve the chicken thighs with the roasted cherries and pearl onions.

moo, baa and oink

IT IS HARD FOR ME to narrow down my favorite food, but easy for me to narrow down my favorite food category—and that is meat, because beef, lamb and pork each has a unique flavor and texture. Also, each cut of meat requires different cooking techniques. I feel that this challenges me and fuels my creativity as a chef.

One of the challenges of cooking meat on a weeknight is that, unless it's a steak, many cuts require a significant amount of time to prepare. And most of us don't want to wait hours for dinner. However, with some essential small kitchen appliances, you can indulge in fall-off-the bone Slow Cooker Tamarind Sticky Ribs (page 68) or the French classic Instant Pot Beef Bourguignon (page 80) any night of the week.

If you're in the mood for a Mediterranean meal, you will delight in my Herb Lamb Chops with Roast Eggplant Israeli Couscous Salad (page 62). It is a beautiful dish that is simple enough to prepare on a weeknight but elegant enough to serve at a dinner party. The lamb is roasted with a fresh herb rub and served with a salad of roasted eggplant, Israeli couscous, fresh herbs and a light dressing.

Of course, no meat chapter is complete without a really great steak. In this chapter, I will share how to prepare Perfect Herb and Butter New York Strip (page 87). There is a great deal of elegance and simplicity in meat and butter. We all need a great steak recipe in our life.

Are you in the mood to level up your Taco Tuesday? I suggest you try my Mole Pork Tacos (page 75). Nuggets of pork tenderloin are rubbed with a mixture of mole, chipotle pepper and Mexican hot chocolate. They are broiled until caramelized and served in warm tortillas with your choice of toppings. Make extra for some killer rice bowls.

I know chicken is the go-to weeknight protein, but I hope these recipes inspire you sear a steak and braise some ribs.

herb lamb chops with roast eggplant israeli couscous salad

1 tbsp (15 ml) olive oil, for pan

Chops
8 rib lamb chops

2 tbsp (30 ml) olive oil

1 tbsp (15 ml) red wine vinegar

2 tsp (scant 2 g) fresh thyme

1 tsp minced fresh rosemary

8 fresh mint leaves, minced

4 cloves garlic, minced

2 tsp (12 g) kosher salt

Salad
1 (1-lb [455-g]) eggplant

⅓ cup (80 ml) + 2 tbsp (30 ml) olive oil, divided, plus more for drizzling

1 tsp kosher salt, plus more for sprinkling

SERVES 4

Hands down, this is one of my favorite dishes. It's simple, so it's a perfect weeknight dinner, but it has enough panache to serve at a dinner party. The eggplant and lamb chops roast on a sheet pan for perfectly browned eggplant and cooked lamb. They are then served with a salad of Israeli couscous, fresh herbs and a light dressing.

Preheat the oven to 425°F (220°C) and adjust a rack to the center of the oven. Line a rimmed sheet pan with foil and brush the pan with the olive oil.

Season the chops: In a resealable plastic bag, combine the lamb chops, olive oil, vinegar, thyme, rosemary, mint, garlic and salt. Seal and shake the bag until the chops are evenly coated, then set aside.

Prepare the salad: Peel strips off the eggplant skin, using a vegetable peeler, leaving some strips of skin for color and texture. Dice the eggplant into 1-inch (2.5-cm) cubes and spread onto the prepared sheet pan. Drizzle the eggplant with 2 tablespoons (30 ml) of the olive oil and sprinkle with the teaspoon of salt. Toss the eggplant until evenly coated with olive oil and salt.

Roast the eggplant in the oven for 10 minutes and then stir, using a spatula. Return the eggplant to the oven and roast for another 10 minutes.

(continued)

8 oz (225 g) dried Israeli pearl couscous

½ cup (15 g) packed fresh mint leaves, roughly chopped

1 cup (62 g) packed fresh parsley leaves, roughly chopped

12 oz (340 g) roasted red pepper, diced

½ medium red onion, small diced

Juice of 1 lemon

2 cloves garlic, grated

Minced fresh mint and parsley, for garnish

NOTES: The lamb chops can be seasoned and stored in the refrigerator in a resealable plastic bag the night before.

The couscous salad can also be prepared and dressed in advance, minus the eggplant, mint and parsley leaves. Lightly reheat the salad, covered, for 1 minute in a microwave and add the fresh herbs before serving.

While the eggplant roasts, prepare the couscous according to the package directions. Fluff the couscous with a fork, drizzle with olive oil to keep from sticking and set aside.

Lower the oven temperature to 400°F (200°C). Stir the eggplant again and arrange it to make space to fit the lamb chops directly on the lined sheet pan. Remove the seasoned chops from the plastic bag and place them on the pan, then return the pan to the oven and roast for 8 to 10 minutes, or until the lamb chops reach an internal temperature of 140°F (60°C).

While the lamb roasts, heat a large stainless-steel or cast-iron skillet over high heat. Remove the lamb chops and eggplant from the oven and sear the lamb chops in the hot skillet for 1 to 2 minutes per side. Return the lamb to the sheet pan to rest outside the oven.

In a large bowl, combine the couscous, roasted eggplant, mint, parsley, roasted red pepper, onion, lemon juice, remaining ⅓ cup (80 ml) of olive oil and the garlic. Toss the salad until well combined. Season with salt to taste.

Serve the lamb chops with the roast eggplant couscous salad and garnish with minced fresh herbs.

slow cooker mulled wine short ribs

5 lbs (2.3 kg) short ribs (about 6 ribs)

Salt and freshly ground black pepper

3 small onions, peeled

2 celery ribs

2 medium carrots

1 head garlic, peeled

2 tbsp (30 ml) olive oil

2 sprigs rosemary

4 or 5 fresh sage leaves

8 sprigs thyme

2 cups (475 ml) red wine (Malbec or merlot)

1 cup (240 ml) beef bone broth or stock

SERVES 4 TO 6

You will be amazed how, with a little planning and a slow cooker, you can have tender short ribs any night of the week. This recipe does require some light prep: sautéing the vegetables and searing the ribs before setting them in the slow cooker to cook overnight. But it is pretty much smooth sailing after that. See the notes for more detailed prep time–saving strategies.

Do not deny yourself these delicious short ribs. Not to mention sauce that is rich in flavor and warm spices. The ribs are wonderful served with Instant Pot Anchovy Butter Whipped Potatoes (page 125), Crispy Rosemary and Beef Tallow Potatoes (page 121), Roast Sweet Potatoes with Tahini Dressing (page 117) or Crispy Roasted Brussels Sprouts with Jalapeño Honey (page 114). Also, serve any leftovers shredded over Creamy Brown Butter Tortellini (page 26).

Sprinkle the short ribs on all sides with salt and pepper. In a food processor, combine the onions, celery, carrots and peeled garlic and pulse to mince.

Set a slow cooker to sauté and heat the olive oil in the slow cooker until simmering, about 1 minute. If your slow cooker doesn't have a sauté feature, heat a large skillet over medium-high heat.

Working in batches, brown the short ribs on all sides, about 2 minutes per side, then transfer to a plate. Add the minced vegetable mixture to the slow cooker (or skillet, if using). Sauté until the onions are tender and the mixture is fragrant, scraping up any brown bits from the bottom of your cooking vessel.

Tie the rosemary, sage and thyme into a piece of cheesecloth to create an herb sachet. If working in a skillet, transfer the vegetable mixture to the slow cooker. Add the short ribs, sachet of herbs, wine and bone broth and cover. Set the slow cooker on low for 8 hours or high for 4 hours.

(continued)

2 tbsp (16 g) cornstarch

¼ cup (60 ml) apple brandy

2 tbsp (30 ml) pure maple syrup

1 cinnamon stick

2 whole cloves

1 whole star anise

3 strips orange zest

Freshly grated nutmeg, for sprinkling

NOTES:

I recommend preparing the ribs the night before and setting the slow cooker to cook overnight. The following morning, refrigerate, uncovered, in the slow cooker crock. When you return in the evening, a fat cap will have formed. Spoon off and discard the fat, then bring the ribs to a simmer, covered, in the slow cooker, stirring occasionally to prevent burning. Once simmering, remove the ribs from the slow cooker and continue with the recipe as written.

See the recipe for Instant Pot Roasted Bone Broth (page 162) to make your own.

Once the slow cooker is done cooking, transfer the short ribs to a serving platter. Strain the liquid through a strainer and into a fat separator. Once the fat has floated to the top, carefully pour the liquid into the slow cooker, leaving behind the fat. Discard the herb sachet.

Spoon out ¼ cup (60 ml) of the liquid and whisk in the cornstarch until smooth and well combined, to make a slurry. Set aside.

Add the apple brandy and maple syrup. Create a spice sachet of the cinnamon stick, cloves, anise and orange zest and add that to the slow cooker. Stir to combine and set to simmer for 15 minutes. During the last 5 minutes, add the slurry and mix until well combined. The sauce will begin to thicken. Return the short ribs to the slow cooker to reheat them.

Serve the short ribs with the sauce, lightly sprinkled with freshly grated nutmeg.

slow cooker tamarind sticky ribs

Ribs
2 slabs baby back ribs

¼ cup (24 g) Chinese five-spice powder

2 tbsp (24 g) ground coriander

2 tsp (12 g) kosher salt

2 tsp (2 g) crushed red pepper flakes

¼ cup (60 g) light brown sugar

Sauce
1 tbsp (15 ml) tamarind concentrate

1 cup (240 ml) water

1 tsp Asian fish sauce

¼ cup (60 g) light brown sugar

1 tsp sesame oil

3 cloves garlic, minced

1 tbsp (8 g) cornstarch

N O T E : The ribs can be seasoned with rub the night before. Cover the ribs and refrigerate until ready to place in the slow cooker the next day. The tamarind glaze can also be prepared ahead and stored in an airtight container in the refrigerator until ready to use.

SERVES 4

Ribs are the original meat on a stick, and who doesn't love meat on a stick? But it takes hours in the oven or in a smoker to get tender ribs. And weeknights are not for babysitting an oven or smoker—this is when a slow cooker comes in handy.

All you have to do is quickly rub the ribs with a mixture of Chinese five-spice powder and brown sugar, then drop them into the slow cooker in the morning and go about your day. The ribs cook in the slow cooker for 4 or 8 hours until they are fall-off-the-bone tender. Brush them with an easy sweet and tart tamarind glaze and broil until sticky. The end result is tender, sweet and tangy ribs. Pair them with Edamame Succotash (page 133) or Roast Carrots with Gochujang Glaze (page 118).

Prepare the ribs: Remove the membrane on the back of the ribs by using a paring knife to pry up the corner of the membrane and gripping it tightly to pull it away. You can use a clean paper towel to help maintain your grip. It is important to remove the membrane, so the ribs are tender and not chewy.

In a small bowl, combine the Chinese five-spice powder, coriander, salt, red pepper flakes and brown sugar. Rub the dry rub on both sides of the rib racks and place them in a 7-quart (6.6-L) slow cooker. It is okay if you need to stack the ribs. Cook on low for 8 hours or high for 4 hours.

Line a rimmed sheet pan with foil and place a rack in it; set aside.

Prepare the sauce: In a small saucepan, whisk together the tamarind concentrate, water, fish sauce, brown sugar, sesame oil and garlic until well combined. Transfer 2 tablespoons (30 ml) of the tamarind mixture to a small bowl, add the cornstarch and mix together until well combined, to create a slurry.

Bring the saucepan of the tamarind mixture to a simmer. Add the slurry to the saucepan and whisk. Let simmer for 1 minute, or until the sauce thickens and coats the back of a spoon.

Set your oven broiler to low and transfer the ribs to the prepared sheet pan, back side up. Brush the ribs with half of the sauce and broil until bubbly and brown, 2 to 3 minutes. Flip the ribs and repeat. Once they're finished broiling, slice the ribs and serve.

herb pork chops with blackberry sauce

Pork Chops

1 tbsp (15 ml) olive oil

1 tsp minced fresh sage

2 tsp (1 g) minced fresh rosemary

1 tsp fresh thyme

2 tsp (12 g) kosher salt

2 cloves garlic, grated

2 tsp (10 ml) white balsamic vinegar

4 (1" [2.5-cm])-thick bone-in rib pork chops

¼ cup (30 g) all-purpose flour

2 tbsp (28 g) salted butter

Sauce

¼ cup (40 g) minced shallot

2 cloves garlic, minced

1 tbsp (2 g) fresh thyme, plus more for garnish

½ cup (120 ml) red wine

½ cup (120 ml) chicken stock

2 pt (600 g) blackberries, plus more for garnish (optional)

2 tbsp (30 ml) honey

1 cinnamon stick

2 tbsp (28 g) salted butter

Kosher salt

SERVES 4

I absolutely love a thick, juicy, bone-in pork chop; it is satisfyingly primal. These garlic and herb pork chops are quickly seared in a hot skillet and finished off in the oven. While the pork chops are in the oven, an easy sweet and tangy blackberry and red wine reduction is prepared in the same skillet. The end result is perfectly cooked pork chops with an elegant touch, in about 30 minutes. Pair these juicy pork chops with Instant Pot Anchovy Butter Whipped Potatoes (page 125) or Crispy Rosemary and Beef Tallow Potatoes (page 121).

Prepare the pork chops: Preheat the oven to 400°F (200°C) and line a rimmed sheet pan with foil.

In a small bowl, combine the olive oil, sage, rosemary, thyme, salt, garlic and vinegar. Stir until well mixed, then rub the mixture onto the pork chops. Pour the flour onto a plate and lightly dredge the chops in the flour, dusting off any excess flour, then transfer to a plate.

Heat a 12-inch (30-cm) stainless-steel skillet over medium-high heat and melt the butter in the skillet. Cook the chops for 3 minutes per side, working in batches if necessary, so as not to crowd the pan. Transfer the chops to the prepared sheet pan (reserving the skillet for the sauce) and bake for 15 minutes, or until the internal temperature reaches 145°F (63°C), then remove from the oven and let the pork chops rest for 5 minutes.

While the pork chops are in the oven, prepare the sauce: To the skillet the pork chops were cooked in, add the shallot, garlic and thyme and sauté for 1 minute, or until fragrant. Deglaze the skillet by adding the wine and scraping up any brown bits. Add the stock, berries, honey and cinnamon stick to the skillet. Simmer the blackberries until they begin to break down, 8 to 10 minutes, and use the back of a spoon to crush the berries.

Place a fine-mesh strainer over a heat-safe bowl and strain the sauce. Return the sauce to the skillet and simmer for 4 to 5 minutes to thicken. Add the butter and whisk until smooth and shiny. Season with salt to taste.

Serve the pork chops with the sauce, garnished with fresh berries (if using) and minced thyme.

spiced lamb meatballs and harissa-spiced yogurt dipping sauce

Yogurt Dipping Sauce

1 cup (230 g) Greek yogurt

1 tbsp (15 ml) harissa paste

1 (2" [5-cm]) piece English cucumber

3 cloves garlic, grated

Leaves from 3 sprigs mint

1 tsp ground cumin

Kosher salt

Meatballs

1 small white onion

3 cloves garlic

6 sprigs thyme

2 sprigs mint

3 sprigs oregano

½ tsp paprika

1 tsp ground coriander

½ tsp ground cumin

1 tsp kosher salt

1 lb (455 g) ground lamb

3 tbsp (21 g) plain dried bread crumbs

1 large egg

NOTES: If you can't find lamb, you can use ground sirloin beef instead. The meatballs can be prepared ahead of time, flash frozen and stored in a resealable plastic bag. Bake for an additional 5 to 10 minutes if frozen.

The yogurt dipping sauce can also be served as an appetizer with vegetables or pita bread.

SERVES 4

If you have never had lamb before, these meatballs are a great introduction. The ground lamb is mixed with Mediterranean herbs, aromatics and spices, resulting in a beautiful savory and slightly sweet flavor combination that complements the lamb—all inspired by the flavors of gyro.

I've paired the meatballs with a harissa-spiced yogurt sauce to provide a little tang and heat. Serve the meatballs in a pita bread wrap, over your favorite whole-grain rice or with my Mediterranean Tomato Salad with Za'atar Pita Chips (page 122).

Preheat the oven to 400°F (200°C). Line a rimmed sheet pan with foil and place a rack in the pan; set aside.

Prepare the yogurt dipping sauce: In a food processor, combine the yogurt, harissa, cucumber, garlic, mint leaves and cumin. Process until well mixed and smooth. Season with salt to taste. Transfer the sauce to a small bowl.

Prepare the meatballs: Without cleaning out the bowl of the food processor, add the onion, garlic, thyme, mint, oregano, paprika, coriander, cumin and salt and pulse until the vegetables and seasonings are finely minced. Scrape down the sides with a spatula. Add the ground lamb, bread crumbs and egg and pulse until the mixture is well combined.

Scoop the lamb mixture onto the rack of the prepared sheet pan, using a 2-tablespoon (30-ml) cookie scoop, leveling each scoop. Then, roll each scoop into an individual ball and bake for 15 to 20 minutes, or until the meatballs are cooked through.

Serve the meatballs with the yogurt dipping sauce.

WHAT'S THAT INGREDIENT? Harissa is a North African condiment. It is made from Baklouti or serrano peppers, garlic, plus such spices as caraway, coriander and cumin. Treat harissa like your favorite hot sauce. Add it to chicken wings, dips, eggs or pasta.

mole pork tacos

¼ cup (60 ml) chicken stock

¼ cup (63 g) prepared mole

1 chipotle pepper

½ tab (46 g) Mexican hot chocolate, such as the Abuelita brand, roughly chopped

1 tsp kosher salt

2 lbs (905 g) pork tenderloin, silver skin removed, cubed into 1" (2.5-cm) pieces

8 to 12 tortillas

Toppings

Avocado, pitted, peeled and sliced

Thinly sliced radish

Fresh cilantro

Small-diced red onion

NOTE: Marinate the pork in the mole the day before to allow more flavor to develop.

SERVES 4 TO 6

Mole is a thick, dense sauce made from a combination of chiles, tomatoes, sugar, spices, nuts, seeds and sometimes chocolate. It is traditionally used as a sauce, but for this recipe, I decided to use it as a wet rub.

Mole has a long list of ingredients and takes a while to prepare. To save time, I use a store-bought mole for this recipe. The pork is rubbed with a mixture of mole, chipotle pepper and Mexican hot chocolate. It is then broiled until browned and caramelized. It is great served as tacos or on a burrito bowl.

Set your broiler to high. Line a large rimmed sheet pan with heavy-duty foil and set aside.

In a blender or food processor, combine the chicken stock, mole, chipotle pepper, Mexican hot chocolate and salt. Blend until well mixed and smooth.

In a large bowl, toss the pork with the mole mixture until evenly coated. Spread out the pork on the prepared sheet pan, doing your best not to crowd the pan.

Broil the pork for 10 minutes. While the pork is in the oven, warm the tortillas in a microwave or lightly char them over a gas flame on the stovetop.

Serve the pork in the warmed tortillas, garnished with your desired toppings, such as avocado, radish, cilantro and red onion.

instant pot braised lamb with apricots and dates

2 lbs (905 g) cubed lamb meat (from shoulder or leg)

½ tsp paprika

1 tsp ground cumin

2 tsp (12 g) kosher salt

¼ cup (30 g) all-purpose flour

3 tbsp (42 g) ghee

1 small onion, small diced

4 cloves garlic, minced

½ cup (120 ml) white wine

1 cup (240 ml) beef bone broth

1 (14.5-oz [411-g]) can diced tomatoes

½ preserved lemon (see note), or zest of 1 lemon, minced

10 dried apricots

10 dried pitted dates

1 (½" [1.3-cm]) piece fresh ginger

1 cinnamon stick

3 whole allspice berries

2 whole cloves

8 coriander seeds

Fresh cilantro, for serving

NOTE: Preserved lemon can be purchased online and at many gourmet grocery stores in the international foods aisle. See the recipe for Preserved Lemons (page 166) to make your own.

SERVES 4 TO 6

I love a great braised lamb dish. This one is inspired by a lamb tagine I ate one time at an Indian restaurant when I lived in Washington, D.C. It usually takes hours of braising to get the lamb tender and infused with flavor, but if you use an Instant Pot or other multifunction cooker, the lamb braises in a fraction of the time. This dish is loaded with spices, tender lamb and hidden nuggets of dried fruit. Serve over rice or with a warm piece of naan.

In a large bowl, combine the cubed lamb, paprika, cumin, salt and flour. Toss until well mixed and the lamb is evenly coated.

Heat a 12-inch (30-cm) stainless-steel skillet over medium-high heat. (I prefer to use a skillet for this step, instead of the sauté feature of an Instant Pot, as it has a larger flat cooking surface.) Melt the ghee in the skillet and then, working in batches, sear the lamb on all sides until browned, about 10 minutes. Transfer the lamb to the Instant Pot.

Lower the heat to medium and add the onion and garlic to the hot skillet. Sauté the onion until softened. Add the wine to the skillet to deglaze the pan, scraping up any remaining brown bits. Transfer the wine and the onion mixture to the Instant Pot.

Add the bone broth, diced tomatoes, preserved lemon, apricots and dates to the Instant Pot. Use a piece of cheesecloth to make a sachet of the ginger, cinnamon stick, allspice berries, cloves and coriander seeds. Mix everything together until well combined.

Set the Instant Pot to cook at high pressure for 20 minutes. Once done cooking, open the valve to release the pressure. Remove the cover and set to simmer for 10 minutes. Remove the sachet and serve the braised lamb garnished with cilantro.

instant pot classic bolognese

2 tbsp (30 ml) olive oil

2 medium carrots, small diced

1 medium onion, small diced

2 celery ribs, small diced

3 sprigs oregano, minced

6 fresh basil leaves, chopped

1 tbsp (4 g) minced fresh parsley

4 cloves garlic, chopped

1 tsp kosher salt

1 tsp anchovy paste

1 lb (455 g) 80/20 ground beef

1 (28-oz [800-g]) can crushed
tomatoes

2 tbsp (30 ml) tomato paste

¼ cup (60 ml) red wine

2 bay leaves

12 oz (340 g) dried pasta

Fresh Parmesan cheese, for serving
(optional)

SERVES 6

You may think that "Bolognese" means simply "meat sauce," but it is so much more. It can take hours of simmering and stirring on the stovetop to accomplish the right texture of traditional Bolognese. The goal is for the meat to be tender and have a deep, rich flavor. But with an Instant Pot or other multifunction cooker, you can enjoy tender Bolognese in a fraction of the time. Serve it over pasta with a side of crusty bread for a complete, comforting meal.

Set an Instant Pot to sauté. Place the olive oil and carrots in the Instant Pot and cook until the carrots are lightly browned, about 5 minutes. Add the onion and celery and cook for 3 minutes, or until the onions and celery are translucent. Add the oregano, basil, parsley, garlic, salt and anchovy paste, then cook, stirring, until well combined and fragrant, about 1 minute.

Add the ground beef and cook for 5 minutes, or until lightly browned and crumbly. Add the crushed tomatoes, tomato paste, wine and bay leaves and stir until well incorporated. Cover and set the Instant Pot to cook at high pressure for 30 minutes.

About 10 minutes before the Bolognese is ready, prepare the pasta according to the package directions. Once the Bolognese is finished cooking, allow the pressure to release naturally for 10 minutes before venting. Serve the Bolognese over the pasta and garnish with Parmesan, if desired.

instant pot beef bourguignon

3 strips thick-cut bacon, diced

2 tbsp (30 ml) water

2 lbs (905 g) stew beef, diced into ½"
(1.3-cm) pieces

3 tbsp (24 g) all-purpose flour

2 tsp (12 g) kosher salt

¼ tsp freshly ground black pepper

3 tbsp (42 g) salted butter, divided

4 carrots, diced

1 cup (137 g) frozen pearl onions

8 oz (225 g) button mushrooms,
quartered

4 cloves garlic, chopped

½ cup (120 ml) red wine

1 tbsp (15 ml) tomato paste

½ cup (120 ml) beef stock

1 tbsp (8 g) cornstarch

SERVES 6

Bust out your best Julia Child impersonation because it's time to make beef bourguignon. *Beef bourguignon* means "beef Burgundy," in reference to the winemaking regions of Burgundy, France.

Traditionally the beef stews on the stovetop for hours, but this beef bourguignon is prepared far faster in an Instant Pot or other multifunction cooker with red wine, carrots, mushrooms and onions. Serve the beef bourguignon with Instant Pot Anchovy Butter Whipped Potatoes (page 125), tender egg noodles, roasted baby potatoes or crusty bread for the perfect French meal.

Set an Instant Pot to more sauté. Place the bacon and water in the Instant Pot. Let the bacon cook, stirring occasionally, until it begins to brown, about 5 minutes.

In a large bowl, combine the beef, flour, salt and pepper. Toss until the beef is evenly coated, then set aside.

Using a slotted spoon, remove the bacon from the Instant Pot and set aside. Add 2 tablespoons (28 g) of the butter to the Instant Pot and stir until melted. Add the floured beef and let cook undisturbed for 3 minutes, or until the beef is lightly browned. Stir the beef and let it cook undisturbed for another 3 minutes, or until the bottom of the pot develops brown bits. Using a slotted spoon, transfer the meat back to the bowl.

Add the remaining tablespoon (14 g) of butter and the carrots, pearl onions, mushrooms, garlic and bacon to the Instant Pot and sauté for 4 minutes. Add the wine, tomato paste and stock to deglaze the pot by scraping up the brown bits from the bottom. Return the browned beef to the pot and stir. Cover and cook at high pressure for 30 minutes. Once done cooking, let the pressure release naturally for 10 minutes before venting.

In a small bowl, whisk together the cornstarch and 3 tablespoons (45 ml) of the broth from the beef bourguignon until well combined. Add the slurry to the beef bourguignon, set the Instant Pot to more sauté and let simmer for 5 minutes to thicken.

slow cooker crispy five-spice pork

1 (3- to 4-lb [1.4- to 1.8-kg]) boneless pork butt, cut into large cubes

Juice of 2 limes

¼ cup (60 ml) sesame oil

¼ cup (60 ml) vegetable oil, plus 2 tbsp (30 ml) for pan, divided

¼ cup (63 g) miso paste

2 tbsp (12 g) Chinese five-spice powder

¼ cup (60 ml) honey

2 tbsp (16 g) grated fresh ginger

1 large onion, halved and sliced

4 scallions, white part minced and green part chopped into segments about 2" (5 cm) long

SERVES 6 TO 8

If you like a set-it-and-forget-it slow cooker recipe, you will love this one. Chunks of pork butt slow cook all day with Chinese five-spice powder and miso paste until tender. By the evening, it is ready to crisp in a hot skillet and sauté with onions. The result is tender pork with wonderfully crispy edges. Serve in tortillas with shredded napa cabbage or with white rice. It also pairs well with the Edamame Succotash (page 133) and Roast Carrots with Gochujang Glaze (page 118).

In a slow cooker, combine the pork, lime juice, sesame oil, ¼ cup (60 ml) of vegetable oil, miso paste, Chinese five-spice powder, honey and ginger, then mix well. Set the slow cooker on medium for 8 hours overnight or in the morning to cook throughout the work day, so the meat is ready by dinnertime.

When the pork is done, heat a 12-inch (30-cm) nonstick skillet over medium-high heat, then heat 1 tablespoon (15 ml) of the vegetable oil for about 30 seconds, or until shimmery. Add half of the sliced onion and the minced white parts of the scallions and sauté for 2 minutes.

Increase the heat beneath the skillet to high. Using a slotted spoon or tongs, transfer half of the pork to the skillet. Press the pork down into the hot pan and allow it to crisp and brown, about 2 minutes. Add half of the scallion greens and drizzle with some of the juices from the slow cooker. Toss until the scallions have wilted, then transfer the pork mixture to a platter. Repeat with the remaining vegetable oil, pork and scallion greens, then transfer to the platter and serve.

WHAT'S THAT INGREDIENT? Miso paste is a Japanese seasoning made from fermented soybeans that are mixed with salt and *koji*, a mold used to make sake. The paste may also include barley, rice, rye or other grains. It can be found in a plastic tub or jars in the refrigerated section of Asian grocery stores, or next to refrigerated tofu in large grocery stores and natural food stores.

skirt steak with orange and shallot gremolata

SERVES 4

Without a doubt, skirt steak is one of my favorite cuts of steak, because it is flavorful and the edges get crispy. Also, it requires only a few minutes to cook, making it perfect for dinner on a weeknight. This skirt steak is rubbed with a simple seasoning of fresh herbs, garlic and brown sugar. It is then pan seared until browned and served thinly sliced, topped with an orange and shallot gremolata. It is light and fresh with just a hint of sweetness.

I recommend mincing the gremolata ingredients by hand instead of using a zesting blade or food processor. This will make for an evenly sized mince and will keep the gremolata loose.

Skirt Steak
1 tbsp (4 g) fresh oregano
3 cloves garlic, minced
1 tbsp (15 g) light brown sugar
1 tsp crushed red pepper flakes
1 tsp salt
2 tbsp (30 ml) vegetable oil, plus 1 tbsp (15 ml) for searing
1 tsp white wine vinegar
2 lb (905 g) skirt steak, silver skin removed

Gremolata
Zest of 2 navel oranges, peeled with vegetable peeler and minced
Zest of 1 lemon, peeled with vegetable peeler and minced
½ cup (8 g) packed fresh cilantro leaves, minced
1 shallot, minced
1 clove garlic, minced
¼ cup (15 g) packed fresh parsley leaves, minced
1 tbsp (15 ml) olive oil

Prepare the steak: In a bowl, combine the oregano, garlic, brown sugar, red pepper flakes, salt, 2 tablespoons (30 ml) of the vegetable oil and vinegar. Mix well and rub onto the steak until evenly coated, then set aside.

Prepare the gremolata: In a bowl, toss together the orange zest, lemon zest, cilantro, shallot, garlic, parsley and olive oil until well combined.

In a heavy-bottomed 12-inch (30-cm) stainless-steel skillet, heat the remaining tablespoon (15 ml) of vegetable oil over medium-high heat until shimmering hot. Add the steak to the skillet and cook for 2 to 3 minutes per side, for medium-rare.

Transfer the steak to a plate and let it rest for 5 minutes. Slice the steak against the grain and top with the gremolata for serving.

NOTES:
The skirt steak can be seasoned ahead of time and stored, covered, in the refrigerator overnight.

The gremolata can also be prepared ahead of time and stored for up to a week in the refrigerator. It also goes well served over grilled chicken or fish.

perfect herb and butter new york strip

2 (1" [2.5-cm])-thick New York strip steaks

Kosher salt and freshly ground black pepper

¼ cup (55 g) salted butter (½ stick)

1 tbsp (15 ml) olive oil

4 cloves garlic

2 sprigs rosemary

6 sprigs thyme

SERVES 2

Everyone needs a great steak recipe under their belt. And this recipe is pretty straightforward: meat, butter and herbs cooked in a piping-hot cast-iron skillet. It doesn't get simpler or more classic then that. Enjoy the steak as prepared or level it up with homemade Herb Butter or Miso Butter (page 178). Serve the steaks with Crispy Roasted Brussels Sprouts with Jalapeño Honey (page 114) or Crispy Rosemary and Beef Tallow Potatoes (page 121).

Preheat the oven to 375°F (190°C). Pull the steaks from the refrigerator and pat dry with paper towels. Lay the steaks on a paper towel–lined plate to sit at room temperature for 20 minutes.

Heat a 12-inch (30-cm) cast-iron skillet over medium-high heat. Pat the steaks dry again with a fresh paper towel and sprinkle both sides with salt and pepper. Heat the butter and oil in the skillet, swirling until the butter has melted. Add the garlic and the rosemary and thyme sprigs and cook the herbs in the butter until fragrant, about 1 minute.

Add the steaks to the skillet and sear for 3 minutes per side, basting them with the butter mixture while they sear. Transfer the skillet to the oven to roast for 3 to 5 minutes, or until the internal temperature reaches 130°F (54°C), for medium rare.

Transfer the steaks to a plate and let rest for 10 minutes before serving.

the perfect charcuterie board

8 oz (225 g) sliced cured meats (e.g., prosciutto, jamón serrano, jamón iberico, bresaola)

8 oz (225 g) cured sausages (e.g., hard salami, Spanish chorizo, sorpressata, capicola)

4 oz (115 g) hard cheese (e.g., aged Cheddar, Parmesan, Asiago)

4 oz (115 g) semihard cheese (e.g., Manchego, Swiss, provolone)

4 oz (115 g) semisoft cheese (e.g., fontina, Stilton, Gorgonzola)

4 oz (115 g) soft cheese (e.g., Brie, goat, Humboldt Fog brand)

6 oz (170 g) pork or chicken spreads (e.g., pâté, terrine or rilletes)

Fixin's

Fruit spread

Honey

Olives

Nuts

Crackers

Fresh or dried fruit

Quick-Pickled Veggies (page 170)

NOTE: I recommend adding Slow Cooker Pork Rillettes (Rustic Pâté) on page 165 and Quick-Pickled Veggies on page 170.

SERVES 6 TO 8

In my refrigerator, I keep a drawer full of cured meats and cheeses. This way, whenever I don't feel like cooking or when we have unexpected guests, I can quickly assemble a charcuterie board. But I'm not talking about any basic ham and cheese deli platter. I like to curate quality meats and cheese with contrasting textures and flavors. Some of my favorite nights have been out on the patio with a charcuterie board and a bottle of wine. Feel free to mix or match your proteins, cheeses and fixin's. There are no hard-and-fast rules, except to have a variety.

Arrange the cured meats and cheeses on a large cutting board. Set out a few small serving bowls for the pork/chicken spreads, fruit spreads and honey, if using them. Fill any remaining space with items from the fixin's list.

from the sea

IF YOU ARE IN SEARCH of dinners that are easy, versatile and flavorful, I recommend you look to the sea. Seafood does not need a significant amount of time or fussing to be amazing. If you are short on energy or time but still in the mood for an elegant dinner, a seafood dinner is your best bet.

The majority of these recipes use seafood that I like to call "stock seafood." It is seafood that is either frozen or preserved by canning or smoking, such as frozen shrimp, canned sardines, smoked fish and canned lump crabmeat—seafood that you can stock in your kitchen to have on hand for a quick dinner.

One of my favorite dishes prepared with stock seafood is Whipped Ricotta and Sardine Toast (page 95) because it's delicious and requires virtually no cooking. Garlic-rubbed toast is smeared with whipped ricotta cheese and topped with sliced Campari tomatoes, sardines and parsley.

If you want to make some showstopping fresh seafood, hop over to my Whole Roasted Chimichurri Red Snapper (page 92). Whole roasted fish needs minimal prep. All this dish requires is rubbing the entire snapper with chimichurri and roasting in the oven. It pretty much guarantees oohs and aahs when presented at the dinner table.

If I had to pick my personal favorite from among these seafood recipes, it would be my Mussels with Orange, Fennel and Black Olives (page 99). It is the most elegant, easy one-skillet meal. The mussels are steamed in a white wine, orange liqueur and butter sauce. I love how the meaty mussels with this light sweet buttery sauce contrast with the briny olives. Also, don't forget crusty bread to soak up all that delicious sauce. I know many that are hesitant when it comes to seafood, but I hope that these recipes look so amazing that you will run to the seafood counter. Seriously, seafood is the ultimate easy weeknight gourmet dinner.

whole roasted chimichurri red snapper

SERVES 6 TO 8

1 cup (62 g) packed fresh parsley leaves

¼ cup (4 g) packed fresh cilantro leaves

2 tbsp (8 g) fresh oregano leaves

3 cloves garlic

½ cup (120 ml) olive oil

⅓ cup (80 ml) red wine vinegar

1 tsp crushed red pepper flakes

½ tsp kosher salt, plus more for sprinkling

1 (3-lb [1.4-kg]) whole snapper, cleaned and scaled

½ large onion

NOTES: Save time by asking your fishmonger to scale and clean the fish for you. If you have to scale the fish yourself, hold it firmly by the tail and use the back of a knife to scrape the fish against the scales in short, stroking motions to remove them. The scales will fly, so it's best to do in a sink or outside. Finish by rinsing the fish under cool water.

See my leveled-up recipe for Chimichurri (page 173) for how to make and store the condiment in advance.

You may think that whole roast fish is intimidating or challenging to prepare, but you will be blown away with how simple it is. Without a doubt, this is my favorite technique for cooking fish because it's simple and forgiving. Serve the snapper with the Crispy Rosemary and Beef Tallow Potatoes (page 121) or White Bean and Asparagus Salad (page 137).

Preheat the oven to 425°F (220°C) and line a sheet pan with foil.

In a food processor, make the chimichurri by combining the parsley, cilantro, oregano, garlic, olive oil, vinegar, red pepper flakes and salt and then processing until smooth.

Make 4 or 5 parallel cuts on each side of the fish, cutting almost to the bone, then place it on the prepared sheet pan. Season the cavity of the snapper with 2 tablespoons (38 g) of the chimichurri. Rub half of the remaining chimichurri over the snapper, rubbing some of it into the cuts. Sprinkle the snapper with salt.

Splay the belly of the snapper and stuff with the half an onion, cut side down. Stand the snapper on the sheet pan, using the onion to prop it up and curving the tail to stabilize it.

Roast in the oven for 30 minutes, or until the flesh flakes. Transfer the snapper to a platter and serve with the remaining chimichurri, being careful to avoid fish bones while eating.

whipped ricotta and sardine toast

15 oz (425 g) whole-milk ricotta cheese

Zest of 1 lemon

½ tsp kosher salt

4 (½" [1.3-cm])-thick slices crusty Italian batard or round loaf

2 tbsp (30 ml) olive oil, plus more for drizzling

1 whole clove garlic

4 Campari or Roma tomatoes, sliced

1 (4-oz [115-g]) can wild sardines in olive oil, cut in half lengthwise

¼ cup (15 g) torn fresh parsley leaves

Freshly ground black pepper

Maldon salt flakes

SERVES 4

Avocado toast, step aside—there is a new toast in my life: ricotta and sardine. It touches every taste bud: It is crunchy, creamy, tangy, sweet and salty. I admit that, at first, I was skeptical about sardine toast. But the first time I took a bite, I almost moonwalked. Except I can't moonwalk, so that was never going to happen.

Did you have a busy day at the office? I recommend you make yourself whipped ricotta and sardine toast and pour yourself a glass of chilled white wine. You will thank me.

In a food processor, combine the ricotta cheese, lemon zest and salt and process until smooth and creamy. Set the mixture aside until ready to use.

Heat a large, heavy skillet over medium-high heat. Brush the bread slices on both sides with olive oil and place in the skillet. Cook the bread slices for 2 minutes on each side, or until evenly browned and toasted. Lightly rub one side of each toast with the garlic clove.

Spread a thick layer of ricotta cheese on the garlic side of each toast. Top each slice with sliced tomatoes, sardines, parsley, pepper, salt flakes and a drizzle of olive oil.

shrimp and coconut green curry

2 tbsp (30 ml) olive oil

1 small onion, minced

4 cloves garlic, minced

1 tbsp (6 g) minced fresh ginger

1 tbsp (15 ml) lemongrass paste

1 red bell pepper, seeded and julienned

¼ cup (60 g) green curry paste

¼ cup (60 ml) clam juice

1 tbsp (15 ml) Asian fish sauce

1 (13-oz [370-g]) can unsweetened coconut milk

2 baby bok choy, quartered

½ cup (34 g) sliced shiitake mushrooms

1 lb (455 g) 31/40 (large) shrimp, peeled and deveined

Cooked rice or rice noodles, for serving

Fresh cilantro, for garnish

Sliced jalapeño peppers, for garnish

Fresh lime juice, for garnish (optional)

SERVES 4

If you like your dishes fresh, bright, full of flavor and ready in 20 minutes, you will love this recipe. Large shrimp simmers in a flavorful coconut, green curry and lemongrass sauce with baby bok choy. If you like it spicy, add some fresh jalapeños or sriracha.

Heat the oil in a 12-inch (30-cm) stainless-steel skillet over medium heat. Once the oil is hot and shimmering, about 1 minute, add the onion and sauté until it begins to get soft, about 3 minutes.

Add the garlic, ginger, lemongrass and bell pepper. Toss until well mixed and sauté until fragrant and the pepper is bright red, about 3 minutes.

Add the curry paste, clam juice, fish sauce and coconut milk and mix until well combined. Bring the coconut milk mixture to a simmer, then add the bok choy and shiitake mushrooms. Toss to combine and continue to simmer, covered, until the bok choy has started to wilt, about 2 minutes. Then, add the shrimp and cook until the shrimp is opaque, 3 to 4 minutes.

Serve over rice or with rice noodles, garnished with cilantro, sliced jalapeño peppers and a squeeze of lime juice, if desired.

mussels with orange, fennel and black olives

2 tbsp (30 ml) olive oil

1 small red onion, finely diced

1 small fennel bulb, thinly sliced, fronds reserved for garnish

3 cloves garlic

Zest and juice of 1 navel orange, divided

¼ cup (60 ml) white wine

6 tbsp (90 ml) orange liqueur, such as Naranja or Cointreau

3 lbs (1.4 kg) Prince Edward Island mussels, debearded

2 tbsp (28 g) salted butter

¼ cup (25 g) pitted black olives, roughly chopped

SERVES 2

While working at a restaurant, I would end my day with a large bowl of mussels cooked in anise liqueur and white wine. Not only were the mussels delicious, but I enjoyed the process of digging them from the shells and tearing a piece of bread to dip in the sauce. This simple one-skillet dish is inspired by those late-night bowls. The mussels are steamed in a white wine, orange liqueur and butter sauce with the fennel and red onion. They are then tossed with chopped black olives and garnished with fennel fronds. Serve with a crusty artisan bread for dipping into the sauce.

Heat the olive oil in a heavy-bottomed 12-inch (30-cm) stainless-steel skillet with a lid (set lid aside) over medium heat. Add the red onion, sliced fennel bulb, garlic and orange zest. Sauté for 2 minutes, or until the fennel is starting to become tender.

Add the wine to the skillet and allow it to reduce for 1 to 2 minutes. Add the orange liqueur and orange juice and stir. Add the mussels and quickly toss to coat with the sauce. Increase the heat to medium-high and cover. After 2 minutes, stir the mussels and replace the lid. Cook for another 6 to 8 minutes, or until all the mussels have opened. Discard any mussels that have not opened after 10 minutes.

Using a slotted spoon, transfer the mussels to a large serving bowl. Add the butter to the sauce that is still in the skillet. Stir until the butter has melted and been incorporated into the sauce. Pour the sauce over the mussels and sprinkle with the chopped olives and reserved fennel fronds.

slow-roasted lemon butter dill salmon and asparagus

6 tbsp (84 g) salted butter, melted

3 cloves garlic, minced

1 tbsp (15 ml) white wine or white wine vinegar

1 tbsp (15 ml) Dijon mustard

1 tsp fresh lemon juice

2 tbsp (8 g) minced fresh dill

1 tbsp (3 g) minced fresh chives

Olive oil

1 lb (455 g) asparagus, bottoms trimmed

8 small radishes, halved

Kosher salt and freshly ground black pepper

1½ lb (680 g) salmon fillet, skin removed

1 lemon, sliced

4 to 6 tbsp (60 to 90 g) skyr (Icelandic yogurt)

NOTES: See the recipe for Lemon-Dill Butter (page 178) for how to make and store it in advance. Substitute 6 tablespoons (84 g) of the Lemon-Dill Butter for butter, garlic and lemon juice mixture.

You can also garnish the dish with finely minced preserved lemon rind. Preserved lemon can be purchased online and at many gourmet grocery stores in the international foods aisle. See the recipe for Preserved Lemons (page 166) to make your own.

SERVES 4

Slow roasting herb butter salmon over a bed of asparagus spears and radishes is the perfect technique for a whole weeknight meal. The result is beautifully cooked flaky salmon and flavorful spears that are tender but still have a little snap.

Preheat the oven to 275°F (135°C) and line a rimmed sheet pan with foil. In a microwave-safe bowl, combine the butter, garlic, wine, Dijon and lemon juice and microwave at 100 percent power for 50 seconds. Add the dill and chives to the butter and whisk the mixture until well combined, then set aside.

Spread 2 tablespoons (30 ml) of olive oil on the prepared sheet pan. Place the asparagus and radishes on the pan and sprinkle with salt and pepper. Toss the asparagus and radishes to lightly coat with the olive oil, then arrange them in a single layer.

Place the salmon fillets on top of the vegetable mixture. Spoon the butter mixture over the salmon and drizzle over the veggies. Arrange the lemon slices on top of the salmon and sprinkle with salt.

Bake the salmon until just opaque in the center, 30 to 35 minutes.

Serve the salmon with the asparagus, radishes and a dollop of skyr.

smoked salmon tostadas with chamoy

SERVES 4

This is a wonderfully delicious, simple and virtually no-cook dish, making it a great meal to prepare on a warm summer day. Crunchy tostadas are topped with crisp slaw and hot-smoked salmon and drizzled with chamoy sauce, a sweet, spicy, tangy, saucy Mexican condiment made with mango or apricot preserves, chili powder, salt and lime. If you are a real fan of heat, feel free to add some sliced fresh jalapeños.

___

Chamoy

½ cup (160 g) apricot preserves

1½ tsp (4 g) ancho chile powder

Juice of 1 lime

1 tsp crushed red pepper flakes

1 clove garlic, grated

Tostadas

1 tbsp (15 ml) vegetable oil, for pan

1 cup (130 g) frozen sweet corn, thawed

Juice of ½ lime

1 tbsp (15 ml) Mexican crema

4 tsp (20 ml) mayonnaise

½ tsp chili powder

1 tsp cider vinegar

1 tbsp (15 ml) honey

Salt

1½ cups (105 g) shredded red cabbage

1 scallion, sliced

8 tostadas

2 (4-oz [115-g]) hot-smoked salmon fillets, diced

Fresh cilantro, for garnish

1 to 2 red jalapeño peppers, thinly sliced, for garnish (optional)

Prepare the chamoy: In a small saucepan, combine the apricot preserves, ancho chile powder, lime juice, red pepper flakes and garlic. Place over medium heat and whisk until the preserves have dissolved and everything is well mixed and smooth, about 3 minutes. Remove from the heat and set aside to cool and use later.

Prepare the tostadas: Heat a 12-inch (30-cm) stainless-steel skillet over medium-high heat. Heat the vegetable oil in the skillet for about 1 minute, or until hot and shimmery. Add the corn to the skillet and stir to evenly coat with the oil. Cook the corn, stirring occasionally, for 5 minutes, or until browned, then remove from the heat and set aside to cool.

In a large bowl, combine the lime juice, crema, mayonnaise, chili powder, vinegar and honey. Whisk until the dressing is well mixed and season with salt to taste. Add the shredded cabbage, corn and scallion and toss until the slaw is evenly coated with the dressing.

Top the tostadas with the slaw and smoked salmon. Then, drizzle with the chamoy and garnish with cilantro and sliced jalapeño peppers, if desired.

vadouvan shrimp with mango-herb salsa

2 firm, ripe mangoes, pitted and small diced

½ small red onion, thinly sliced

½ cup (15 g) packed fresh mint leaves

½ cup (12 g) packed fresh Thai basil leaves

½ cup (8 g) packed fresh cilantro leaves

1 red jalapeño pepper, seeded and small diced

2 tbsp (30 ml) olive oil

Juice of ½ lime

Kosher salt

1 lb (455 g) 16/20 (extra-jumbo) shrimp, peeled, deveined, tail on

4 tsp (8 g) vadouvan

2 tbsp (28 g) ghee

SERVES 4

Shrimp dishes cook quickly, which makes them a wonderful weeknight option. This shrimp is seasoned with vadouvan, a French colonial–influenced Indian masala curry powder. It's a warm spice blend of classic curry spices, such as fenugreek, cumin, coriander and cardamom, with such aromatics as onion and garlic. It gives the shrimp a mild spicy kick that is complemented with the sweet mango-herb salsa.

In a large bowl, combine the mangoes, red onion, mint, Thai basil, cilantro, jalapeño, olive oil and lime juice. Toss until well mixed, season with salt to taste and set aside.

In a medium bowl, toss the shrimp with the vadouvan until evenly coated. Heat a 12-inch (30-cm) stainless-steel skillet over medium-high heat and melt the ghee in the skillet. Add the shrimp and cook until pink and cooked through, about 6 minutes.

Serve the shrimp with the mango-herb salsa.

smoked trout and rye panzanella

Vinaigrette

1½ tbsp (scant 23 ml) prepared horseradish

1 clove garlic, grated

3 tbsp (45 ml) cider vinegar

1 tbsp (15 ml) buckwheat or clover honey

½ cup (120 ml) olive oil

Panzanella

3 tbsp (45 ml) olive oil

6 cups (300 g) cubed rye bread (from 1 loaf)

1 tsp kosher salt

12 oz (340 g) grape tomatoes, halved

1 English cucumber, seeded, quartered and cut into 1" (2.5-cm) chunks

½ red onion, halved and sliced

3 tbsp (26 g) capers

¼ cup (16 g) packed dill fronds, roughly chopped

8 oz (225 g) smoked trout fillet, flaked

SERVES 6

Panzanella, an Italian salad made of stale bread, tomatoes, onions and cucumbers, is one of my favorite summer salads. This recipe is inspired by it and by a girls' trip to New York City, where we indulged in smoked fish and rye bread. I have swapped out the Tuscan bread for rye bread, added smoked trout and tossed it all in a horseradish vinaigrette. It's an addictive and filling salad, making it perfect as a meal.

Prepare the vinaigrette: In a small bowl, combine the horseradish, garlic, vinegar, honey and olive oil. Whisk until well mixed and emulsified.

Prepare the panzanella: Heat a 12-inch (30-cm) stainless-steel skillet over medium heat. Add the olive oil and cubed bread to the skillet, sprinkle with salt and toss until well combined. Toast the bread in the skillet, tossing frequently, for 10 minutes, or until lightly browned and toasted.

In a large bowl, combine the toasted rye bread, tomatoes, cucumber, onion, capers and dill. Drizzle with the dressing and add the smoked trout. Toss until well mixed and evenly coated with the dressing.

crab and chile mango lettuce wraps

1 lb (455 g) jumbo lump crabmeat

1 mango, pitted and small diced

¼ tsp chili powder

½ tsp ancho chile powder

Zest of ½ lime

3 tbsp (45 ml) fresh lime juice, plus
more to taste

⅓ cup (55 g) small-diced red onion

2 tbsp (30 ml) olive oil

1 cup (16 g) fresh cilantro leaves

1 tsp kosher salt, plus more to taste

1 small Hass avocado, firm but ripe,
peeled, pitted and small diced

Lettuce leaves, for serving

Mexican crema, for drizzling

SERVES 4

Inspired by the Mexican street food of sweet mango flowers with chile, I
thought a lump crabmeat salad with mango, chile and avocado would be
a fabulous light meal. This salad comes together quickly and can be made
ahead for an even easier weeknight meal. I typically serve this salad as a
lettuce wrap, but you can also serve it over salad greens or with tortilla chips.

In a large bowl, combine the crabmeat, diced mango, chili powder, ancho
chile powder, lime zest and juice, red onion, olive oil, cilantro and salt. Toss
until well mixed. Add the avocado and gently mix until it is well incorporated.
Season with more salt and lime juice to taste.

Serve the crabmeat mixture in lettuce leaves, drizzled with Mexican crema.

guava and pineapple shrimp

Sauce

½ cup (160 g) guava marmalade

2 cloves garlic, pressed

Juice of 1 lime

½ tsp crushed red pepper flakes

1 tsp Asian fish sauce

1 tsp soy sauce

Shrimp

2 tbsp (30 ml) vegetable oil

1 red bell pepper, seeded and small diced

½ cup (80 g) small-diced red onion

1 cup (155 g) small-diced pineapple

1½ lbs (680 g) 21/25 (jumbo) shrimp, peeled, deveined, tail on

Salt

Fresh cilantro, for serving

Lime wedges, for serving

SERVES 6

I love guava! It's sweet, it's tangy, it's excellent with cheese and crackers, and it also makes a killer sauce. Shrimp, pineapple and red peppers are sautéed in a sweet and savory guava sauce and finished with cilantro. In 20 minutes, you will be transported to a tropical dining paradise. This dish can be served with white rice or Edamame Succotash (page 133) for a complete meal.

Prepare the sauce: Heat a medium saucepan over medium-high heat. Combine the marmalade, garlic, lime juice, red pepper flakes, fish sauce and soy sauce in the saucepan. Whisk together until well mixed and the marmalade has melted. Let simmer for 4 minutes, then remove from the heat and set aside.

Prepare the shrimp: Heat a 12-inch (30-cm) stainless-steel skillet over medium-high heat. Heat the vegetable oil in the skillet until shimmery, about 1 minute. Add the bell pepper, red onion and pineapple. Cook for 5 minutes, stirring only once or twice to allow the peppers and pineapple to brown and caramelize.

Add the shrimp to the skillet. Cook for 1 minute, then add the guava sauce and cook the shrimp for 3 to 4 minutes, or until done. Season with salt to taste and serve with cilantro and lime wedges.

kicking sidekicks

I KNOW THAT, WHEN PLANNING a meal, a lot of focus is put on the main dish and side dishes are sometimes a fleeting thought. But don't underestimate a great side dish—sometimes it's what makes the meal!

A fabulous side dish is a great way to elevate a simple protein. All of these side dishes are easy to prepare but still have an element of panache. Pair them with your favorite grilled or roasted protein, and dinner goes from good to spectacular. It's not always about the steak; sometimes, it's about the Brussels sprouts.

I have a potato side dish for every kind of potato lover. If you are a fan of sweet and savory, go for my Roast Sweet Potatoes with Tahini Dressing (page 117). If you are in the mood for creamy and salty, check out my Instant Pot Anchovy Butter Whipped Potatoes (page 125). And if you are a fan of crispy potatoes, you will swoon over my Crispy Rosemary and Beef Tallow Potatoes (page 121). All of these potato dishes are so full of flavor yet uncomplicated.

Now, let's talk about vegetables, such as my Crispy Roasted Brussels Sprouts with Jalapeño Honey (page 114), which are roasted at a high temperature and then drizzled with jalapeño honey for a hint of heat. I warn you that they are dangerously addictive.

If you desire a side dish with a bit of protein, you will want my interpretation of pork and beans, Cannellini Beans and Pancetta (page 129). This is a simple one-skillet recipe that cooks in 15 minutes. The white kidney beans simmer in a sauce of white wine, butter and fresh herbs, and are then tossed with crispy pancetta for texture and saltiness. These beans are great served with grilled fish or chicken.

crispy roasted brussels sprouts with jalapeño honey

1 cup (240 ml) clover honey

1 jalapeño pepper, halved and sliced, half of the seeds removed

1 clove garlic, thinly sliced

1½ lbs (680 g) Brussels sprouts, trimmed and halved

¼ cup (60 ml) vegetable oil

½ tsp kosher salt, plus more for sprinkling

½ tsp granulated garlic

1 tsp chili powder

NOTE: Store any remaining jalapeño honey in a sealed container in the refrigerator up to 3 months. Drizzle over all your favorite foods. It's amazing on fried chicken or biscuits. Jalapeño honey can also be prepared in advance to develop more heat.

SERVES 4

Brussels sprouts have gotten a bad rap over the years, but I promise you that if they are prepared correctly, they are as addictive as potato chips. This recipe was inspired by the four rounds of Brussels sprouts my girlfriends and I ordered while out to dinner one night. That's right; we ordered four rounds of Brussels sprouts, not drinks—that is how good they were.

These are so easy, it's almost wrong that they are so freaking delicious. All you need to do is to toss seasoned Brussels sprouts on a hot sheet pan and into the oven. They roast until the leaves are crispy and the center of the sprouts are tender, then they're drizzled with jalapeño-infused honey. Serve with the Perfect Herb and Butter New York Strip (page 87) or Slow Cooker Mulled Wine Short Ribs (page 65).

Adjust 2 oven racks at the top and bottom of the oven. Preheat the oven to 450°F (230°C) and place a rimmed sheet pan on the top rack.

In a small container with an airtight lid, combine the honey, jalapeño and garlic. Stir together until well mixed, then cover and set aside.

In a large bowl, combine the Brussels sprouts, vegetable oil, salt, granulated garlic and chili powder.

Carefully remove the sheet pan from the oven and spread the Brussels sprouts, cut side down, on the pan. Roast on the bottom rack for 15 to 17 minutes, or until the leaves are crispy and the sprouts are tender.

Transfer the Brussels sprouts to a serving platter, drizzle with the jalapeño honey, sprinkle with salt and serve.

roast sweet potatoes with tahini dressing

SERVES 4 TO 6

Potatoes
3 lbs (1.4 kg) sweet potatoes, cut into wedges

¼ cup (55 g) ghee, melted

2 tsp (12 g) kosher salt

2 tsp (5 g) paprika

1 tbsp (8 g) sumac

2 cloves garlic, grated

Fresh cilantro, for garnish

Dressing
¼ cup (60 g) tahini, well bended

¼ cup (60 ml) olive oil

1 tbsp (15 ml) fresh lemon juice

2 cloves garlic, grated

1 tbsp (15 ml) honey

½ tsp kosher salt

First, a warning: These sweet potatoes may not make it to your plate. First time I made them, I picked them right off the sheet pan, dipped them into the dressing and put them straight into my mouth. I love to serve these potatoes with a perfectly cooked steak like the Perfect Herb and Butter New York Strip (page 87) for a twist on the typical steak and potatoes dinner, or with Crispy Za'atar Chicken and Cauliflower (page 41).

Prepare the potatoes: Preheat the oven to 450°F (230°C) and line a rimmed sheet pan with foil.

On the prepared baking sheet, toss the potatoes with the ghee, salt, paprika, sumac and garlic. Roast, tossing occasionally, until tender and browned, about 25 minutes.

While the potatoes roast, prepare the dressing: In a small bowl, whisk together the dressing ingredients until well combined and emulsified. If the dressing is too thick to drizzle, add up to 1 tablespoon (15 ml) of water. Serve the sweet potatoes drizzled with the tahini dressing and garnished with cilantro.

roast carrots with gochujang glaze

Carrots
1½ lbs (680 g) whole carrots
2 tbsp (30 ml) vegetable oil
½ tsp kosher salt
½ tsp ground coriander
Glaze
¼ cup (80 g) gochujang
¼ cup (60 g) light brown sugar
Zest and juice of 1 orange
1 tsp sesame oil
1 tsp low-sodium soy sauce
2 tsp (4 g) minced fresh ginger
2 cloves garlic, minced
2 scallions, thinly cut on the bias

NOTE: The glaze is also great over grilled or roast meats.

SERVES 4

If you like sweet and spicy, you are going to flip for these carrots. The carrots are roasted and coated with a glaze of brown sugar, gochujang, orange and ginger. They are lovely served with the Slow Cooker Tamarind Sticky Ribs (page 68).

Prepare the carrots: Preheat the oven to 475°F (245°C) and line a sheet pan with foil.

Scrub the carrots and cut in half lengthwise (if they are thin, keep whole); there is no need to peel. Place on the prepared sheet pan and drizzle with the vegetable oil. Sprinkle with the salt and coriander. Toss until the carrots are evenly coated, then spread them out in a single layer. Roast in the oven for 10 minutes.

While the carrots roast, prepare the glaze: In a medium saucepan, whisk together the gochujang, brown sugar, orange zest and juice, sesame oil, soy sauce and ginger until well combined.

Place the saucepan over medium-high heat and bring to a low boil. Cook the glaze, stirring occasionally to prevent sticking, for 5 minutes, or until thick bubbles begin to form. Add the garlic and cook for an additional 2 minutes.

Coat the carrots with the glaze and bake for an additional 10 minutes. Transfer the carrots to a platter and serve garnished with the scallions.

WHAT'S THAT INGREDIENT? Gochujang, a red chile paste, is a savory, sweet and spicy condiment made from fermented soybeans. Although it is used in Korean cuisine, it also can be added to barbecue sauce, ketchup, dips, marinades and soups or stews to add some umami and heat.

crispy rosemary and beef tallow potatoes

2 lbs (905 g) russet potatoes (about 3 potatoes), peeled and thinly sliced (see notes)

1 shallot, halved and thinly sliced

1 tsp minced fresh rosemary

1 tsp kosher salt

5 tbsp (70 g) beef tallow, melted (see notes)

SERVES 4 TO 6

What is more classic than beef and potatoes? So, it makes sense to cook sheet pan potatoes in beef tallow, which is rendered beef fat; this produces perfectly crisp potatoes with a light beefy flavor. Pair these crispy potatoes with Grapefruit and Pink Peppercorn Cream Chicken Thighs (page 54) or White Wine–Poached Chicken with Lemon Butter Sauce (page 53).

Place the oven rack at the center of the oven and preheat the oven to 450°F (230°C).

In a large bowl, combine the sliced potatoes, shallot and rosemary and sprinkle with the salt. Toss the potatoes until well coated.

Drizzle the melted beef tallow over the potatoes and quickly toss. The beef tallow may seize a bit, but do not be alarmed; this is normal.

Spread out the potatoes into an even layer on a 15 x 21–inch (38 x 53–cm) rimmed sheet pan. It is okay if some of the potatoes overlap, as long as they are in an even layer.

Bake for 20 minutes. Using a large spatula, gently flip the potatoes and return them to the oven to bake for another 15 minutes, or until browned and very crisp.

Serve while they're hot and crisp.

NOTES:

To slice the potatoes thinly and evenly, use the slicing blade of a food processor or a Japanese mandoline.

Beef tallow can be found jarred in many gourmet or natural food stores; it can also be purchased online. If you cannot find beef tallow, you can use ghee or clarified butter—see the recipe for Clarified Butter, Ghee and Brown Butter (page 179) to make your own.

mediterranean tomato salad with za'atar pita chips

SERVES 4

Pita Chips
4 pita breads, cut into wedges

2 tbsp (30 ml) olive oil

1½ tsp (scant 4 g) za'atar

Dressing
Juice of ½ lemon

¼ cup (60 ml) olive oil

1 tsp salt

1 tsp (scant 4 g) za'atar

Salad
2 lbs (905 g) Campari or Roma tomatoes, quartered

4.5 oz (130 g) capers, drained

¼ cup (40 g) julienned red onion

1 cup (62 g) loosely packed fresh parsley leaves

4 oz (115 g) feta cheese, crumbled

2 tsp (5 g) za'atar

NOTE: Level up by adding 1 tablespoon (18 to 20 g) of minced preserved lemon rind to the dressing. Preserved lemon can be purchased online and in the international foods aisle in many gourmet grocery stores. See the recipe for Preserved Lemons (page 166) to make your own.

Nothing is lighter or fresher than a tomato salad. Sweet Campari tomatoes are quartered and tossed in a lemon dressing with briny capers, peppery red onion, parsley leaves, feta cheese and za'atar. And because I love a crunch, I have paired the salad with toasted za'atar pita chips. Serve this salad with grilled chicken or Spiced Lamb Meatballs and Harissa-Spiced Yogurt Dipping Sauce (page 72).

Prepare the pita chips: Preheat the oven to 375°F (190°C) and line a rimmed sheet pan with foil.

Spread the pita wedges on the prepared sheet pan, drizzle them with the olive oil and sprinkle with the za'atar. Toss the pita wedges until they are evenly coated. Bake for 10 to 12 minutes, or until lightly browned and crisp.

While the pita chips are in the oven, prepare the dressing: In a large bowl, whisk together the lemon juice, olive oil, salt and za'atar until well combined.

Prepare the salad: Add the tomatoes, capers, red onion, parsley, feta cheese and za'atar to the bowl of dressing. Toss until combined and evenly coated with dressing.

Serve the salad over the pita chips.

instant pot anchovy butter whipped potatoes

2 lbs (905 g) Yukon Gold potatoes, unpeeled, diced into 2" (5-cm) cubes

1 cup (225 g) salted butter (2 sticks), at room temperature

4 cloves garlic, pressed

2 tbsp (8 g) chopped fresh parsley

1 tbsp (15 ml) anchovy paste

½ tsp salt

¼ cup (60 ml) heavy cream

SERVES 6

Why boil your potatoes and lose flavor and starch when you can steam them and make the creamiest, most potatoey mashed potatoes?

When steamed in an Instant Pot or other multifunction cooker, the potatoes cook quickly and emerge tender. They are then whipped with anchovy and butter, resulting in creamy, salty potatoes with a hint of umami. Trust me—you will be putting anchovies into all your foods after this. Pair these mashed potatoes with Perfect Herb and Butter New York Strip (page 87), Instant Pot Beef Bourguignon (page 80) or Slow Cooker Mulled Wine Short Ribs (page 65).

Pour 1 cup (240 ml) of water into an Instant Pot. Add a steamer basket. If you don't have a steamer basket, place parchment paper over the rack insert. Place the diced potatoes in the steamer basket and set to cook on high for 10 minutes. Once done cooking, release the pressure valve.

In a large bowl, combine the potatoes, butter, garlic, parsley, anchovy paste, salt and cream. With a hand mixer, whip the potatoes until fluffy.

crispy broccoli with lemony yogurt

Broccoli

2 heads broccoli, cut into long-stemmed florets

2 tbsp (30 ml) olive oil

2 tsp (12 g) kosher salt

2 tsp (5 g) paprika

3 cloves garlic, minced

Yogurt Sauce

1 cup (230 g) whole-milk Greek yogurt

Zest of 1 lemon

1½ tsp (scant 8 ml) fresh lemon juice

2 cloves garlic, grated

½ tsp paprika

Kosher salt

SERVES 4

I say everyone should eat broccoli, especially this broccoli. The florets roast until they are crisp and the stems are tender. I have paired them with a tangy yogurt sauce that balances broccoli's bitter notes. Serve with grilled fish, chicken, the Crispy Za'atar Chicken and Cauliflower (page 41) or Ras el Hanout Chicken with Prune and Olive Tapenade (page 50).

Prepare the broccoli: Preheat the oven to 475°F (245°C) and lined a rimmed sheet pan with foil.

In a large bowl, toss the broccoli with the olive oil, salt, paprika and garlic until well combined and evenly coated. Spread the broccoli florets in a single layer on the prepared sheet pan. Roast in the oven for 30 minutes.

While the broccoli roasts, prepare the yogurt sauce: In a small bowl, whisk together the yogurt, lemon zest and juice, garlic and paprika until well combined, season with salt to taste, then set aside until ready to use.

Serve the broccoli with the lemony yogurt.

cannellini beans and pancetta

8 oz (225 g) pancetta, diced

½ small onion, small diced

1 tsp minced fresh sage, plus more for garnish

1 tsp minced fresh rosemary, plus more for garnish

3 cloves garlic, minced

¼ cup (60 ml) white wine

¼ cup (60 ml) chicken stock

1 tbsp (15 ml) Dijon mustard

2 (15.5-oz [439-g]) cans cannellini beans, drained and rinsed

1 tbsp (14 g) salted butter

Fresh lemon juice, to finish

SERVES 4

This dish is my fancy play on pork and beans. It is loaded with flavor and comes together in a matter of minutes. Cannellini beans are one of my favorite beans, due to their creamy texture. This is a wonderful side for grilled chicken breast or fish, such as grilled halibut or cod, or the Slow-Roasted Lemon Butter Dill Salmon and Asparagus (page 100).

Heat a 12-inch (30-cm) stainless-steel skillet over medium heat and add the pancetta and 1 tablespoon (15 ml) of water to the skillet. Cook the pancetta for 6 to 7 minutes, or until it is crispy and the fat has rendered.

Transfer the pancetta to a paper towel–lined plate. Then, drain the drippings into a heatproof glass and add 2 tablespoons (30 ml) of pancetta drippings back to the skillet. If there are any drippings left, they can be discarded. Add the onion to the skillet and sauté until translucent, 2 to 3 minutes.

Add the sage, rosemary and garlic to the skillet and sauté until fragrant. Add the wine to deglaze the skillet, scraping up any brown bits in the pan. Then, add the chicken stock, Dijon and beans. Quickly stir everything together until well combined.

Bring the liquid to a boil, then lower the heat to a simmer. Simmer, uncovered, for 3 to 4 minutes, or until the sauce has reduced by half. Add the butter to the skillet and toss with the beans until the butter is melted and well incorporated.

Squeeze the lemon juice over the beans, toss, then garnish with minced fresh sage and rosemary.

potato salad with fresh herb vinaigrette

3 lbs (1.4 kg) petite potatoes, rinsed and halved

¼ cup (60 ml) white wine vinegar

6 tbsp (90 ml) olive oil

1 tsp anchovy paste

¼ cup (15 g) fresh dill leaves

¼ cup (6 g) fresh basil leaves

¼ cup (15 g) fresh parsley leaves

1 scallion, sliced

SERVES 6

This potato salad is one of my favorites, so much so that I make it often for dinner. The tender, petite potatoes are tossed in a light, fresh herb vinaigrette. But the best part is, because the potatoes steam in a microwave, this salad takes less than 10 minutes to prepare and can be served with a variety of dishes. Serve with the Perfect Herb and Butter New York Strip (page 87), Whole Roasted Chimichurri Red Snapper (page 92) or White Wine–Poached Chicken with Lemon Butter Sauce (page 53).

In a large, microwave-safe bowl, combine the potatoes and add ¼ cup (60 ml) of water. Cover the bowl tightly with plastic wrap and microwave at 100 percent power for 7 minutes. The potatoes should be fork-tender but still firm. If they aren't done, continue to microwave them in 20-second increments.

While the potatoes steam, prepare the dressing: In a small bowl, combine the vinegar, olive oil and anchovy paste and whisk until emulsified.

Drain the potatoes and toss the warm potatoes with the dressing, dill, basil, parsley and scallion.

edamame succotash

12 oz (340 g) frozen shelled edamame

4 slices bacon, diced

1 small onion, diced

1 cup (110 g) French-cut fresh green beans

3 cloves garlic, minced

3 cups (450 g) fresh corn kernels (from 4 ears)

1 tbsp (15 ml) Asian fish sauce

2 tsp (10 ml) sriracha

1 tbsp (15 ml) sesame oil

12 oz (340 g) grape tomatoes, halved

2 scallions, sliced

¼ cup (10 g) loosely packed fresh Thai basil leaves, minced, plus more for garnish (optional)

Juice of ½ lime

Salt

NOTE: I keep a bag of shelled frozen edamame on hand in the freezer, so I can easily prepare this dish. Not to mention, they are a great addition to stir-frys, salads and soups.

SERVES 4 TO 6

I will be honest—for the longest time, I had no idea what succotash was. I thought it was something that a cat would declare during my Saturday morning cartoons. Little did I know it's a delicious bean salad.

This recipe is a Thai twist on that traditional American side dish. Lima beans have been replaced by edamame, which are tossed with a fish sauce dressing and garnished with Thai basil. You'll be eating this salad all summer long. Serve this salad with Slow Cooker Tamarind Sticky Ribs (page 68) or Slow Cooker Crispy Five-Spice Pork (page 83).

Steam the edamame in their bag according to the package directions, then set aside.

Heat a large cast-iron or heavy-bottomed stainless-steel skillet over medium heat. Cook the diced bacon in the skillet until crispy and the fat has rendered, about 8 minutes. Using a slotted spoon, transfer the bacon to a paper towel–lined plate to drain. Reserve the bacon drippings in the skillet.

Add the onion, green beans and garlic to the skillet. Cook, stirring often, until the onion is tender, about 6 minutes.

Add the corn, edamame, fish sauce, sriracha and sesame oil. Continue to cook, stirring often, until the corn is bright yellow, about 5 minutes. Stir in the bacon, tomatoes, scallions, Thai basil and lime juice. Toss everything together until well combined and season with salt to taste. Garnish with additional Thai basil, if desired.

charred zucchini with pesto

Pesto

1 cup (24 g) packed fresh basil leaves

¼ cup (15 g) packed fresh parsley leaves

1 clove garlic

Zest of 1 lemon

1 tsp fresh lemon juice, plus more for serving

2 tbsp (18 g) pine nuts

½ cup (120 ml) olive oil

1 tsp salt

¼ cup (25 g) shredded Parmesan cheese, plus more for serving

Zucchini

6 medium zucchini, quartered and cut in half

3 tbsp (45 ml) olive oil

½ tsp kosher salt

¼ tsp granulated garlic

¼ tsp crushed red pepper flakes

SERVES 4

One of the first side dishes I ever blogged about was a side dish of roasted zucchini and peppers. I loved the simplicity of the recipe, but more so, the flavor of roasted and slightly charred vegetables. The zucchini are broiled until evenly charred and then served topped with a garlicky pesto. You can enjoy these as a side dish or serve them tossed with pasta and All the Herbs Roast Chicken Breast (page 57) for a complete meal.

Place an oven rack one space down from the broiler and set the broiler to high. Line a rimmed sheet pan with foil and set aside.

Prepare the pesto: In a food processor, combine the pesto ingredients and process until smooth, then set aside.

Prepare the zucchini: Spread the cut zucchini on the prepared sheet pan. Drizzle with the olive oil and sprinkle with the salt, granulated garlic and red pepper flakes. Toss until the zucchini is evenly coated, then arrange, skin side down, in a single layer.

Broil the zucchini, tossing once, for 2 to 5 minutes, or until charred. Serve drizzled with the pesto, sprinkled with Parmesan and garnished with a little fresh lemon juice.

white bean and asparagus salad

SERVES 4 TO 6

⅓ cup (80 ml) olive oil

½ tsp lemon zest

3 tbsp (45 ml) fresh lemon juice

2 tsp (10 ml) honey

2 tbsp (20 g) minced shallot (about 1 small shallot)

1 tsp white wine vinegar

½ tsp kosher salt

1 bunch asparagus (about 1 lb [455 g])

2 (15.5-oz [439-g]) cans cannellini beans, drained and rinsed

½ cup (30 g) chopped fresh parsley leaves, plus more for serving (optional)

6 fresh basil leaves, torn, plus more for serving (optional)

¼ cup (25 g) shaved Parmesan cheese, plus more for serving (optional)

NOTES: The salad can be made a day ahead and stored in an airtight container in the refrigerator.

Level up by grating Cured Egg Yolks (page 169) over the salad or garnishing with finely minced Preserved Lemons (page 166).

Tender cannellini beans and crunchy raw asparagus coins are tossed with a lemony dressing, rounded out with salty Parmesan cheese and fresh herbs. It's a salad of simple ingredients and bright flavors. It is excellent paired with the White Wine–Poached Chicken with Lemon Butter Sauce (page 53) or All the Herbs Roast Chicken Breast (page 57). You can also serve this salad topped with a runny fried or poached egg.

In a large bowl, whisk together the olive oil, lemon zest and juice, honey, shallot, vinegar and salt until well combined and emulsified.

Trim away the tough ends of the asparagus. Fill a bowl with ice water and set aside. Pour ¼ cup (60 ml) of water into a 2-quart (2-L) casserole dish. Lay the asparagus in a single layer in the dish and cover with plastic wrap. Microwave on high for 1½ minutes, remove the wrap and stir, recover the dish and microwave again for another 1½ minutes. Quickly transfer and submerge the asparagus in the ice bath. Then, lay the cooled asparagus on clean paper towels and pat dry.

Cut the asparagus on the bias into ½-inch (1.3-cm) rounds. Transfer the asparagus to the bowl of dressing and add the beans, parsley, basil and Parmesan. Toss until well combined. Garnish with more parsley, basil and Parmesan, if desired, and serve.

sweet endings

THE END OF A MEAL is the last memory you have of that meal, the final taste that lingers on your palate. Because of this, I always believe it is a must that a fabulous dinner needs an equally fabulous dessert. Dessert is dinner's punctuation mark, and my goal is that these desserts are worthy of exclamation points.

It is important to me that all these desserts be amazing, but it's equally vital that they are easy. Each of these desserts requires a short amount of time to put together or can be made in advance to enjoy throughout the week. Because everyone deserves dessert every night of the week.

If you are a chocolate lover, you must try the Cherry and Dark Chocolate Galette (page 140). This dessert serves the classic pairing of cherries and dark chocolate in a crisp free-form tart. For this recipe, I recommend using your favorite store-bought piecrust to make it especially easy.

Another simple dessert that is gourmet and worthy of a boldface exclamation point is the Red Wine–Poached Figs with Whipped Mascarpone (page 148): fresh Black Mission figs gently poach in spiced Malbec until just tender, then are served with whipped mascarpone. This dessert is rich without being heavy.

Microwaves aren't just for reheating leftovers; they are also great for making the Upside-Down Peach-Ricotta Microwave Cake (page 151). These soft little cakes, topped with caramelized peaches, cook in just minutes. The ricotta and lemon zest give them a slight tang that balances beautifully with the caramelized peaches.

There is a dessert to satisfy every sweet tooth. Whether you're a fan of fruit, chocolate or citrus desserts, this chapter holds a treat for you.

cherry and dark chocolate galette

12 oz (340 g) frozen dark cherries, halved

2 tbsp (26 g) granulated sugar

1 tbsp (8 g) cornstarch

1 tbsp (15 ml) corn syrup

1 tsp almond extract

½ cup (88 g) dark chocolate chips

Prepared dough for 1 single piecrust

3 tbsp (45 ml) heavy cream or half-and-half

3 tbsp (45 g) light brown sugar

SERVES 8

If you love pie but don't have a pie pan, there is no need to fret because there is galette. Yeah, I just rhymed because a dessert this tasty and easy deserves a poem to be written about it.

A filling of cherry, almond and dark chocolate is wrapped in a piecrust that is sprinkled with brown sugar. The classic flavor pairings and free-form crust give this dessert an elegant rustic touch.

Preheat the oven to 400°F (200°C).

In a large bowl, combine the cherries, sugar and cornstarch. Stir the cherries until evenly coated. Add the corn syrup, almond extract and chocolate chips and mix until well combined.

Carefully roll out the piecrust on a sheet pan lined with parchment paper. Spoon the cherry mixture into the center of the piecrust. Spread out the cherry mixture, leaving a 2-inch (5-cm) bare margin around the crust. Bring the edges of the crust over the fruit, folding it over the cherry mixture.

Brush the crust with the cream and sprinkle with the brown sugar.

Bake for 25 to 30 minutes, or until the crust is golden brown. Remove from the oven and let the galette cool completely on a wire rack before serving.

sweet plantain and coconut whipped cream crepes with dulce de leche

½ cup (120 ml) vegetable oil

2 ripe plantains, peeled and sliced on the bias

½ cup (120 ml) heavy cream

2 tbsp (25 g) granulated sugar

½ cup (120 ml) coconut cream

4 store-bought crepes

½ cup (120 ml) store-bought dulce de leche

Powdered sugar, for dusting (optional)

NOTES:

For this recipe, you need well-ripened plantains—they should be mostly black with some yellow spots. If you cannot find ripe plantains and don't have the patience for green plantains to ripen, you can purchase "platanos maduros" in the frozen food section of some grocery stores. Prepare the plantains according to the package directions and assemble the crepes.

The coconut cream can be scraped from the fat cap of full-fat canned coconut milk. Although some stores now carry canned coconut cream, it is not to be confused with cream of coconut, which is found in the drink mix aisle.

SERVES 4

I always say, wrap anything in a crepe and you instantly feel fancy. Even a humble sweet plantain. I grew up eating fried sweet plantains. Sometimes, we would eat them as a side to a savory dish or for dessert with ice cream, similar to bananas Foster.

Inspired by this childhood treat, I thought to give a Spanish Caribbean twist to bananas Foster. Ripe sweet plantain slices are lightly fried until golden and caramelized, then wrapped in a crepe with dulce de leche and topped with coconut whipped cream.

In a large, heavy skillet, heat the vegetable oil over medium-high heat. Carefully place a slice of plantain into the oil. If the oil immediately begins to bubble, it is ready for frying. If it does not bubble, let it heat for another 1 to 2 minutes. Working in batches, cook the plantain slices for 3 to 4 minutes per side, or until golden brown and caramelized. Transfer the plantains to a paper towel–lined plate.

In a large bowl, combine the cream and granulated sugar. Using a hand mixer, beat to stiff peaks. Gently fold the coconut cream into the whipped cream. Set aside.

Reheat the crepes according to the package directions. Spread 2 tablespoons (30 ml) of the dulce de leche on each crepe. Lay 3 to 4 plantain slices on top of the dulce de leche. Fold each crepe in half and then fold its sides over to form a wedge. Dust the crepes with powdered sugar if desired, using a fine-mesh strainer, and top with a dollop of coconut whipped cream.

polenta budino with strawberry-rhubarb compote

Budino
3 cups (710 ml) whole milk

1 cup (175 g) quick-cooking polenta

6 tbsp (78 g) granulated sugar

½ cup (115 g) light brown sugar

¼ cup (60 ml) honey

2 tbsp (28 g) salted butter

Zest of 1 lemon

½ cup (120 ml) heavy cream

2 large egg yolks

Compote
1 lb (455 g) frozen rhubarb

1 lb (455 g) frozen strawberries

¼ cup (50 g) granulated sugar

2 tbsp (30 ml) honey

Juice of 1 lemon

Ice cream, for serving

NOTE: The budino and compote can be stored in airtight containers in the refrigerator. When serving the budino, stir to loosen it, then top with the compote.

SERVES 6

Everyone needs sweet cornmeal pudding in their life, and polenta budino is here to deliver. Polenta is cooked with milk, cream, eggs and sugar to make a rich, creamy cornmeal pudding. This recipe uses quick-cooking polenta so the budino cooks in a matter of minutes. I serve it with a strawberry and rhubarb compote. The sweet cornmeal pudding balances out the tart strawberry-rhubarb compote.

Prepare the budino: In a medium saucepan, bring the milk to a boil. Lower the heat and slowly whisk in the polenta. Cook, whisking constantly, until thick and smooth, about 5 minutes. Whisk in the granulated and brown sugars and honey until well combined. Remove from the heat and add the butter and lemon zest.

In a small bowl, whisk together the cream and egg yolks until well combined. Add the mixture to the polenta and whisk vigorously until well combined. Transfer the polenta to a casserole or shallow dish and cover with plastic wrap, laying the plastic wrap directly over the polenta. Set aside to cool.

Prepare the compote: In a large saucepan, combine the rhubarb, strawberries, granulated sugar, honey and lemon juice. Mix well, cover and place over medium heat. Let it cook for 5 minutes to thaw and juice the frozen fruit. Uncover the fruit and stir, then increase the heat to a simmer. Cook, uncovered, for 15 minutes, or until the mixture begins to thicken. Remove from the heat and set the compote aside to cool.

To serve, stir the polenta to loosen it, then serve with the compote and ice cream.

tahini bread pudding with vanilla sauce

SERVES 6 TO 8

During a girls' trip to New York City, I had my first taste of *halvah*, a crumbly tahini and honey confection from the Middle East. I had always thought of sesame as a savory ingredient, but halvah showed me it also works in sweets. Adding tahini to the custard adds a creamy texture and gives this bread pudding a nutty flavor that cuts into the overt sweetness of typical bread pudding. Serve it warm with vanilla sauce and, if you are feeling extra indulgent, a scoop of vanilla ice cream.

Prepare the bread pudding: Preheat the oven to 350°F (180°C) and butter a 4- to 6-cup (1- to 1.4-L) baking dish.

Spread out the cubed brioche in a single layer on a sheet pan and place it in the oven. Bake for 5 minutes, or until the brioche is lightly toasted and dry. In a large bowl, combine the eggs, milk, tahini, granulated sugar and honey to create a custard. Spread the toasted brioche cubes in the casserole dish and pour the custard over the bread.

Gently toss the brioche with the custard and let it sit for about 5 minutes to allow the bread to soak up the custard. Bake for 30 to 40 minutes, or until set. While the bread pudding bakes, prepare the sauce: In a medium saucepan, combine the butter, white and brown sugars, heavy cream and vanilla. Whisk over medium heat until melted and smooth, then set aside.

Serve the bread pudding warm with the sauce.

Bread Pudding
Salted butter, for baking dish

1 loaf brioche bread, 1½" (4 cm) cubed (makes about 5 to 6 cups [250 to 300 g] of bread crumbs)

3 large eggs

2 cups (475 ml) whole milk

¼ cup (60 g) tahini

¼ cup (50 g) granulated sugar

¼ cup (60 ml) honey

Sauce
½ cup (112 g) salted butter (1 stick)

½ cup (100 g) granulated sugar

½ cup (115 g) light brown sugar

½ cup (120 ml) heavy cream

1 tbsp (15 ml) vanilla extract, or the seeds of 1 vanilla bean

NOTES:

The bread pudding can be assembled in advance. Cover the dish with plastic wrap, store it in the refrigerator overnight and then bake it the following morning.

Leftovers can be sliced and stored in an airtight container in the refrigerator for up to 5 days. It can be enjoyed cold, at room temperature or warmed.

red wine–poached figs with whipped mascarpone

Whipped Mascarpone
8 oz (225 g) mascarpone cheese

2 tbsp (30 ml) heavy cream

2 tsp (10 ml) honey

Figs
1 strip orange zest

1 cup (240 ml) Malbec wine

½ cup (100 g) sugar

1 cinnamon stick

3 sprigs thyme

1 tbsp (15 ml) vanilla extract

1 tbsp (15 ml) honey

8 large Black Mission figs

NOTES:
This dessert can be made ahead, and the components can be stored in airtight containers in the refrigerator for up to 1 week.

It is important to use Black Mission figs, as other kinds of figs are not as sweet.

SERVES 4

I know this recipe sounds super fancy, but it's the easiest of all desserts. Fresh figs are poached in a sweetened red wine mixture that is then reduced to a syrup. The figs are paired with sweetened whipped mascarpone and drizzled with the wine reduction. It's a wonderfully light and sweet dessert—the perfect end to a hearty meal, such as the Instant Pot Classic Bolognese (page 79).

Prepare the whipped mascarpone: In a medium bowl, combine the mascarpone, cream and honey. Using a hand mixer, whisk until creamy and fluffy, then set aside.

Prepare the figs: Using a vegetable peeler, peel a strip of zest from the orange. In a large saucepan, combine the wine, sugar, cinnamon stick, thyme, vanilla, honey and orange zest. Over medium-high heat, bring the wine to a boil. Lower the heat to a simmer, then add the figs. Simmer for 8 to 10 minutes, or until the figs are tender but not mushy.

Using a slotted spoon, remove the figs from the poaching liquid. Increase the heat and bring the wine mixture to a boil. Boil, uncovered, for 7 to 10 minutes, or until syrupy.

Serve the figs, cut in half, with the whipped mascarpone and drizzle with the wine syrup.

upside-down peach-ricotta microwave cake

Cooking spray, for ramekins

Topping
2 tbsp + 2 tsp (40 ml) melted salted butter

¼ cup (60 g) light brown sugar

1 cup (250 g) diced frozen peaches

Cakes
6 tbsp (84 g) unsalted butter (¾ stick), melted

½ cup (100 g) granulated sugar

¼ cup (60 ml) whole milk

1 tsp vanilla extract

1 tsp lemon zest

¼ cup (65 g) whole-milk ricotta cheese

1 large egg

1 tsp baking powder

½ tsp salt

¾ cup (94 g) all-purpose flour

Quick Caramel Sauce
3 tbsp (42 g) salted butter

2 tbsp (26 g) granulated sugar

1 tsp heavy cream

SERVES 4

Whoever said you can't make a fabulous cake in the microwave? These wonderfully tender little cakes come together in a matter of minutes and then are topped with sweet caramelized peach slices. No one will ever believe these petite treats are cooked in the microwave.

Spray 4 (6-oz [177-ml]) ramekins with cooking spray.

Prepare the topping: In a medium bowl, combine the melted butter and brown sugar; mix until the brown sugar is well incorporated. Divide the butter mixture equally among the 4 ramekins. Arrange the diced peaches in the bottom of each of the ramekins.

Prepare the cakes: In the same bowl, whisk together the butter, granulated sugar, milk, vanilla, lemon zest, ricotta and egg until well combined. Add the baking powder, salt and flour and stir until just incorporated. Evenly divide the cake batter among the prepared ramekins.

Microwave at 100 percent power each individual ramekin for 2½ minutes, or 2 ramekins at a time for 6 minutes, or until the cake tests clean with a toothpick inserted into its center.

Invert each cake onto a dessert plate.

Prepare the caramel sauce: In a small bowl, combine the butter, granulated sugar and cream. Microwave at 100 percent power for 30 seconds and whisk until well mixed. Drizzle over the cakes and serve.

brown butter apple tarte tatin

SERVES 8

5 tbsp (70 g) salted butter

¾ cup (150 g) sugar

1 tbsp (15 ml) vanilla extract

1 tbsp (15 ml) cider vinegar

5 to 6 small Granny Smith apples (1½ lbs [680 g]), peeled, cored and quartered

1 sheet puff pastry, thawed

All-purpose flour, for dusting

Vanilla ice cream or whipped cream, for serving

You can never go wrong with an apple dessert, and this one is a winner. If you have never had a tarte Tatin, think of it as an upside-down skillet pie. The brown butter and apple cider vinegar caramel sauce gives the apples a deep, rich flavor. And my favorite part is the sticky caramelized puff pastry edges. I love my slice with a scoop of vanilla bean ice cream.

Preheat the oven to 375°F (190°C).

In a stainless-steel skillet, melt the butter over medium-high heat. You want to use stainless-steel so you can see the butter solids brown. Keeping a close eye on the butter, cook it until it begins to bubble and brown, stirring occasionally to keep it from scorching, about 5 minutes.

Pour the browned butter into a 10-inch (25-cm) cast-iron skillet. Add the sugar, vanilla and vinegar. Whisk together until well combined. Heat the skillet over medium heat. Once the sugar begins to simmer, cook for 5 minutes. Remove the skillet from the heat and carefully arrange the apples in the skillet in a circular pattern. It's best if you crowd the apples, as they will shrink when cooked.

Cook the apples over medium heat for 10 minutes. They will begin to release their juices. If the sauce begins to get too dark, lower the heat.

While the apples are cooking, remove the puff pastry from the refrigerator. Unfold the pastry and, using the lid of a 10-inch (25-cm) skillet as a guide, cut a circle from the puff pastry. Lightly dust the puff pastry with flour and, with a rolling pin, roll out the puff pastry circle until ½ inch (1.3 cm) thick. Once the apples have finished cooking, carefully rearrange the apples in a circular pattern. Then, lay the puff pastry over the apples and tuck it in around the sides of the skillet.

Place the skillet in the oven and bake, rotating halfway through, for 15 minutes, or until the puff pastry is fully puffed and golden brown. Remove from the oven and set the tarte Tatin aside to rest for 10 to 15 minutes.

Lay a rimmed serving platter over the skillet and carefully invert the tarte Tatin onto it. Slice and serve the tarte Tatin with vanilla ice cream or whipped cream.

mexican hot chocolate pots de crème

⅔ cup (160 ml) heavy cream

⅓ cup (80 ml) whole milk

2 tabs Mexican hot chocolate, such as the Abuelita brand, chopped

½ cup (88 g) bittersweet chocolate chips

4 large eggs

1 tbsp (15 ml) vanilla extract

½ tsp ancho chile powder or cayenne pepper

Whipped cream, for garnish (optional)

Ground cinnamon, for garnish (optional)

SERVES 10

Calling all chocolate lovers: You are going to go weak in the knees over these—little cups of spiced chocolate that sets until thick and creamy. The best part is that with a blender and some hot cream, these come together in a matter of minutes. Make them early in the week and you'll be treating yourself all week long.

In a small saucepan, heat the cream and milk over medium-high heat until just about to boil, about 5 minutes.

Meanwhile, in a blender, combine the Mexican hot chocolate, chocolate chips, eggs, vanilla and ancho chile powder. Blend until the chips are smooth and the eggs are well blended.

With the blender running on low speed, slowly add the hot cream mixture to the chocolate mixture and blend until smooth. Pour equal amounts of the mixture into 10 (3-ounce [90-ml]) shot glasses and refrigerate for 4 hours, or until set. Then, cover with plastic wrap and keep refrigerated until ready to serve.

Garnish with whipped cream and cinnamon before serving, if desired.

blackberry and peach ginger clafoutis

¼ cup (55 g) unsalted butter (½ stick), melted, divided

1 cup (240 ml) whole milk

3 large eggs

½ cup (100 g) sugar

2 tsp (10 ml) vanilla extract

1½ tsp (scant 2 g) ground ginger

½ cup (60 g) all-purpose flour

1 pt (300 g) blackberries

1 peach, pitted and sliced

Vanilla ice cream, whipped cream or powdered sugar, for serving

NOTE: Clafoutis can be made ahead, sliced and stored in an airtight container for up to a week. Reheat in the microwave for 1 minute and serve with vanilla ice cream or whipped cream, or dusted with powdered sugar.

SERVES 8

Clafoutis is a French dessert of black cherries baked in a simple egg batter, poured into a baking dish and topped with fresh fruit and baked until browned. I like to describe it as a custardy fruit pancake. I opted to stray from the traditional and make this clafoutis with blackberries, peaches and a hint of ginger. It can also double as a sweet breakfast dish.

Preheat the oven to 325°F (160°C). Coat a 10-inch (25-cm) cast-iron skillet with 2 tablespoons (30 ml) of the melted butter and set aside.

In a blender, combine the milk, eggs, sugar, vanilla, remaining 2 tablespoons (30 ml) of melted butter, ginger and flour. Blend until well mixed and smooth. Pour into the prepared skillet and top evenly with the fruit.

Bake for 40 minutes, or until set and golden brown around the edges. Remove from the oven and set the skillet aside to cool. Then, slice and serve with vanilla ice cream or whipped cream, or dusted with powdered sugar.

lavender and meyer lemon pound cake

SERVES 6 TO 8

Cake

Unsalted butter and all-purpose flour, for pan

2 cups (400 g) sugar

Zest of 5 Meyer lemons (about ¼ cup [24 g] zest)

½ cup + 1 tbsp (126 g) unsalted butter, at room temperature

½ cup (120 ml) honey

⅓ cup (80 ml) fresh Meyer lemon juice (from about 2 lemons)

2 large eggs

3½ tsp (3 g) culinary-grade dried lavender buds

1 cup + 2 tbsp (140 g) all-purpose flour

½ tsp baking powder

½ tsp kosher salt

Glaze

¼ cup (60 ml) heavy whipping cream

1 tbsp (2 g) culinary-grade dried lavender buds

Juice of 1 small Meyer lemon

2½ cups (300 g) powdered sugar

NOTE: When Meyer lemons are not in season, you can replace the zest with 2½ teaspoons (5 g) each of tangerine zest and lemon zest, and the juice with 2½ tablespoons (38 ml) each of fresh lemon juice and tangerine juice.

Lavender is one of the easiest edible flowers to come by, and it goes wonderfully with Meyer lemon. If you like to end your day with a cup of hot tea, this lavender and lemon bread is the perfect treat to pair with it. This cake is light, sweet and delicate. Simply slice off a piece and you have a posh ending to any busy day. The batter and glaze come together quickly and easily. I like to make this cake on the weekend to enjoy all week long.

Prepare the cake: Preheat the oven to 350°F (180°C) and generously butter and flour a nonstick 6-cup (1.4-L) Bundt pan.

In a large bowl, combine the sugar and Meyer lemon zest and rub together until the zest and sugar are evenly mixed. Add the butter and honey and, using a hand mixer, cream the mixture together. Add the Meyer lemon juice, eggs and lavender and beat until well combined. Add the flour, baking powder and salt and beat until just incorporated.

Pour the batter into the prepared Bundt pan. Bake for 35 to 40 minutes, or until the cake tests clean when a toothpick is inserted into it. Remove from the oven and transfer to a wire rack to cool completely.

While the cake bakes, prepare the glaze: In a small saucepan, bring the cream to a simmer over medium-high heat, then remove from the heat. Add the lavender to the cream and let steep while the cake cools. Once the cake cools, pour the lavender mixture into a medium bowl and whisk in the lemon juice and powdered sugar until well combined and smooth.

Invert the cake upright back onto its wire rack and set the rack on a sheet of parchment paper. Pour the glaze over the cake.

leveling up by making ahead

THIS LAST CHAPTER IS ALL about the art of making ahead. I have chosen some key condiments and components that are great to have on hand in a weeknight gourmet kitchen. This way, you can take even the simplest dish and turn it up a notch. It's what I like to call leveling up a dish.

If you want to add a little brightness and bite, consider adding some pickled red onion or cucumber (page 170). If you want a mildly tart lemony flavor with your salad, toss in some minced Preserved Lemons (page 166). One of the best ways to turn up the volume on a dish is to add a hit of acid.

Have you ever experienced the magic of Cured Egg Yolks (page 169)? Now is the time. I love to grate a little over my salads, avocado toast or a pasta dish. Salt-cured egg yolks are a great way to add a little salt and creaminess to your favorite dish.

If you love butter—and who doesn't?—I have all the butter variations covered in this chapter (pages 178 to 181). They include trusty clarified butter and its nuttier counterpart, ghee, both of which have a 482°F (250°C) smoke point, plus my personal favorite, brown butter, with all of its deliciously caramelized brown bits. Not to mention four different compound butters: miso, anchovy, herb and lemon dill.

If spreadable pork butter sounds amazing, I suggest you pull out your slow cooker to make pork rillettes (page 165), a rustic French pork pâté of pork shoulder that slow cooks in pork fat until it falls apart. Spread it in the Chicken and Pâté Banh Mi (page 42), on toast with pickled red onion, or add it to The Perfect Charcuterie Board (page 88). I call for each of these recipes throughout *Weeknight Gourmet Dinners*. But the great thing is that they can be used in virtually any recipe. Add roasted garlic (page 177) to your favorite mac and cheese, fry an egg in herb butter (page 178), or add a dollop of pesto (page 174) to your polenta. The possibilities are endless.

instant pot roasted bone broth

2 lbs (905 g) beef marrow bones or rotisserie chicken bones

2 lbs (905 g) oxtail or chicken wings

¼ cup (60 ml) red wine (if making beef broth) or white wine (if making chicken broth)

2 unpeeled carrots, cut into 2" (5-cm) pieces

1 large onion, quartered

1 medium leek, halved, chopped and rinsed

1 head garlic, halved crosswise

2 ribs celery, chopped

3 bay leaves

MAKES 8 CUPS (1.9 L) BONE BROTH

If you have ever wondered what the difference is between stock and bone broth, it essentially comes down to the amount of time it cooks. Bone broth cooks longer than stock, breaking down the collagen in the bone and connective tissue. The end result is a rich broth that has a silky texture. A bone broth can take up to 24 hours to cook on the stovetop, but with an Instant Pot or other multifunction cooker, you can have bone broth in a fraction of the time. This bone broth can be used in any recipe that calls for stock or bone broth, such as the Ginger Chicken Meatball Ramen (page 45), Mole Pork Tacos (page 75), Instant Pot Beef Bourguignon (page 80), Slow Cooker Mulled Wine Short Ribs (page 65) and Instant Pot Braised Lamb with Apricots and Dates (page 76).

Preheat the oven to 450°F (230°C) for beef broth or 400°F (204°C) for chicken broth. Spread the bones and wings on a rimmed baking sheet and roast in the oven for 30 minutes.

Quickly transfer the bones to a 6-quart (5.7-L) Instant Pot. If preparing beef broth, pour the red wine into the hot baking sheet; if preparing chicken broth, use the white wine. Deglaze the pan, scraping the brown bits from the sheet pan. Spoon the wine in the pan over the bones and add the remaining ingredients. Add enough water to reach the maximum fill line, about 8 cups (1.9 L).

Set the Instant Pot to cook for 5 hours on high pressure for beef broth and 3½ hours on high pressure for chicken broth. Once the timer goes off, let the pressure release naturally.

Strain the bone broth into a large bowl to remove the bones and vegetables. Pour the broth into a fat separator and carefully pour into gallon-sized (4-L) food storage containers. If you don't have a fat separator, you can refrigerate overnight and remove the fat cap from the broth once it has solidified.

The bone broth can keep in the refrigerator for up to a week or for 6 months if frozen.

slow cooker pork rillettes (rustic pâté)

MAKES 6 TO 7 CUPS (1.1 TO 1.3 KG) RILLETTES

3 lb (1.4 kg) boneless pork butt, cut into 2" (5-cm) pieces

2 tsp (3 g) allspice berries, crushed

3 juniper berries, crushed

2 tsp (3 g) black peppercorns, crushed

½ tsp coriander seeds, crushed

¼ cup (72 g) kosher salt

Leaves from 10 sprigs thyme

8 cloves garlic, peeled and crushed

2 (14-oz [397-g]) jars pork leaf lard, melted

2 bay leaves

¼ cup (60 ml) white wine

Pork rillettes is a rustic pâté of pork that is prepared confit style, which means it was cooked and preserved in fat. It has to cook at a low temperature for a long period of time. Instead of having the oven on all day, I like to start prepping the night before, then use a slow cooker to cook it the next day.

This recipe requires an overnight marinade and a long slow cook, but it requires little hands-on work. Also, it makes a large quantity that stays good for 6 months, so you will have it on hand whenever you need it.

The pork becomes a creamy spread that is rich with flavor. Serve it spread on toast with pickled onions (page 170), on The Perfect Charcuterie Board (page 88) or in the Chicken and Pâté Banh Mi (page 42).

In a large bowl, toss the pork with the crushed spices and salt until well coated. Toss the thyme and garlic in with the meat. Cover and refrigerate overnight.

Set out the pork on the countertop to come to room temperature. Place the melted lard in a 6-quart (5.7-L) slow cooker along with the pork, bay leaves and wine. Leave the cover of the slow cooker slightly askew—this is to prevent steam from building up in the slow cooker—and cook on low until the meat is very tender, about 5 hours.

Let cool slightly, then, using a slotted spoon, transfer the pork and garlic to a large bowl, discarding the bay leaves. Shred the pork, discarding any gristle. Stir in 1 cup (240 ml) of the fat from the slow cooker. Pack the rillettes into glass jars or individual crocks. Do not seal yet.

Reheat the remaining fat and ladle a ½-inch (1.3-cm)-thick layer on top of the jarred pork, making sure the pork is fully covered. Seal and store in the refrigerator up to 6 months. Discard the remaining fat or strain and save it refrigerated for another use.

preserved lemons

¼ cup (72 g) kosher salt

6 lemons

Fresh lemon juice, if needed

MAKES 6 LEMONS

Preserved lemon is commonly found in Indian and North African cuisine. Lemons are preserved in a salt and lemon juice mixture, making the rind soft and translucent. The pulp can be used in braises and stews, such as the Instant Pot Braised Lamb with Apricots and Dates (page 76); and the rind can be sprinkled over dishes at the end of cooking, such as the Slow-Roasted Lemon Butter Dill Salmon and Asparagus (page 100), to give them a mildly tart and lemony flavor. I love to toss preserved lemon into salad dressings and rice, such as the Peach and Burrata Farro Salad (page 29).

Clean a pint-sized (500-ml) glass jar and lid with hot, soapy water. Dry with a clean towel, place 1 tablespoon (18 g) of the salt in the bottom of the jar, then set the jar aside.

Thoroughly scrub and wash the lemons under hot water and pat dry with a clean towel.

Carefully quarter the lemons, starting from the top to within ½ inch (1.3 cm) of the bottom. Sprinkle the remaining salt into the lemons, coating their flesh. Reshape the lemons to be whole and pack them into the jar.

Using a wooden spoon or pestle, press the lemons down to release their juice. Press out enough juice for the lemons to be submerged in their juice, leaving some air space before sealing the jar. If the lemons don't release enough juice to cover them, add more fresh lemon juice until the lemons are submerged.

Seal the jar and give the lemons a good shake to distribute the salt. Keep the jar in a warm, dry place for 2 weeks, shaking daily to distribute the juice and salt. Then, refrigerate the jar for 1 week, or until the rinds are tender and becoming translucent. Once the lemons are ready, they can be stored in the refrigerator for up to 6 months.

To use the lemons, rinse them under cold water, remove the pulp and mince the rind. The rind can be added at the very end of cooking or used raw. The pulp can be minced and added to simmer in soups and stews.

cured egg yolks

2 cups (400 g) sugar

2 cups (600 g) kosher salt

6 pasture-raised large egg yolks

Cooking spray, for rack

If you have never made cured egg yolks, you need to as soon as possible. The process of curing is so simple: separate the egg yolks, pack in a sugar and salt mixture, wait a week, rinse and dry. The end result is hard egg yolks that are reminiscent of pecorino or Parmesan cheese. Grate cured egg yolk over the Anchovy, Caper and Bread Crumb Pasta (page 25), Instant Pot Risotto à la Carbonara (page 17), Instant Pot Classic Bolognese (page 79), White Bean and Asparagus Salad (page 137), Potato Salad with Fresh Herb Vinaigrette (page 130), or Perfect Herb and Butter New York Strip (page 87).

In a food processor, combine the sugar and salt and pulse 20 times to evenly mix and lightly grind.

Pour half of the salt mixture into an 8 x 10–inch (20 x 25–cm) casserole dish. Make six ¼-inch (6-mm)-deep indentations in the salt mixture. Carefully place the egg yolks into the indentations and cover the yolks with the remaining salt mixture.

Cover the casserole dish with plastic wrap and refrigerate for 1 week. Preheat the oven to 200°F (95°C) and adjust the rack to the center of the oven. Place a wire rack on a rimmed baking sheet. Spray the wire rack with cooking spray and set aside. Fill a bowl with cool water. Carefully remove the yolks from the salt mixture. Brush off any excess salt and rinse the yolks in the water. Pat the yolks dry with a clean paper towel and transfer to the prepared wire rack.

Place the sheet pan in the oven to dry the yolks for 30 to 40 minutes, or until they are dry to the touch.

Grate or thinly slice the yolks into your favorite dish. The cured yolks are great grated over pasta, risotto, salads or buttered toast.

The yolks can be stored in an airtight container for up to 2 weeks.

quick-pickled veggies

8 oz (225 g) vegetables
(e.g., red onion, carrot, green beans,
cucumber)
1 bay leaf
1 clove garlic
1½ tsp (9 g) kosher salt
1 tbsp (13 g) sugar
½ cup (120 ml) white vinegar
1 cup (240 ml) water

MAKES 1 (1-PINT [500-ML]) JAR VEGGIES

I always have some pickled vegetables on hand. I love to add them to salads, sandwiches and charcuterie boards. It's a great and easy way to brighten any dish. Pickled vegetables are used in the White Cheddar Dutch Baby with Arugula and Watercress Salad (page 22), Chicken and Pâté Banh Mi (page 42) and The Perfect Charcuterie Board (page 88).

Wash a pint-sized (500-ml) heatproof glass jar and lid with hot, soapy water and rinse well. Dry the jar with a clean kitchen towel and set aside.

Wash your vegetables of choice thoroughly and prep them: Peel onions or carrots, trim ends off green beans, then cut into your desired shapes and sizes. Pack the vegetables into the cleaned jar along with the bay leaf and garlic.

In a medium saucepan, combine the salt, sugar, vinegar and water. Bring to a boil over high heat, then lower the heat to a simmer, stirring to dissolve the salt and sugar.

Pour enough liquid into the jar to cover the vegetables, leaving some air space. Tap the jar against the countertop to release any air bubbles. Screw the lid tightly onto the jar. Leave the jar to cool at room temperature and then store in the refrigerator for a minimum of 24 hours before opening. The pickled vegetables will keep in the refrigerator for up to 2 months.

chimichurri

2 cups (125 g) packed fresh parsley
leaves

½ cup (8 g) packed fresh cilantro
leaves

1 tbsp (4 g) fresh oregano leaves

3 cloves garlic, minced

2 tsp (2 g) crushed red pepper flakes

½ tsp kosher salt

½ cup (120 ml) olive oil

1½ tbsp (22 ml) red wine vinegar

MAKES 1 CUP (ABOUT 225 G) CHIMICHURRI

Chimichurri is the herb condiment that should be in everyone's refrigerator. It's an Argentinean blend of minced parsley, oregano, garlic, olive oil and vinegar. It's amazing, and honestly, it is just fun to say. Chimichurri is best served over grilled meats, but I also love it over fish, such as in the Whole Roasted Chimichurri Red Snapper (page 92).

In a food processor, combine the parsley, cilantro, oregano, garlic, red pepper flakes and salt, then pulse until finely chopped. Add the olive oil and vinegar and pulse 5 or 6 times, or until well incorporated.

Transfer the chimichurri to a small, airtight container and store in the refrigerator for up to 3 weeks.

my favorite basil pesto

2 cups (50 g) fresh basil leaves

½ cup (30 g) fresh flat-leaf parsley leaves

4 cloves garlic

Juice of ½ lemon

¼ cup (35 g) pine nuts

1 tsp salt

¼ cup (25 g) shredded Parmesan cheese

¼ cup (60 ml) olive oil

MAKES 1 CUP (260 G) PESTO; 6 TO 8 SERVINGS

Pesto is a delicious and versatile Italian condiment made of basil, Parmesan, pine nuts, salt and olive oil. It's great on almost everything. Toss it into your favorite pasta, spread it on crostini or serve over roast chicken breast. It is also a component of the Charred Zucchini with Pesto (page 134). I use this pesto for a quick dinner, added to warm pasta that I serve with All the Herbs Roast Chicken Breast (page 57) and crusty bread.

In a food processor or blender, combine the basil and parsley leaves, garlic, lemon juice, pine nuts, salt and Parmesan. With the processor or blender running, slowly drizzle in the olive oil through the opening in the lid and blend until smooth and emulsified.

Transfer to small, airtight container and store in the refrigerator for up to 1 week.

For long-term storage, divide the pesto into molds or ice cube trays and freeze. Store the cubes in a resealable plastic bag in the freezer for 3 months. Place in a hot skillet to thaw.

whole roasted garlic

2 large heads garlic

2 tbsp (30 ml) olive oil

1 tsp kosher salt

MAKES 2 LARGE HEADS GARLIC

Roasted garlic is a wonderful thing to have on hand. Roasting it mellows its sharp bite: It becomes soft and buttery, making it a great addition to enhance any meal. I love to add it to pasta dishes, such as the Anchovy, Caper and Bread Crumb Pasta (page 25); spread on the Perfect Herb and Butter New York Strip (page 87); or serve it with crostini on The Perfect Charcuterie Board (page 88).

Preheat the oven to 425°F (220°C).

Rub the garlic heads to remove any loose skin. Cut ¼ inch (6 mm) off the top of each garlic head and place the heads, cut side up, on a sheet of foil. Drizzle 1 tablespoon (15 ml) of the olive oil over each garlic head and sprinkle with the salt.

Wrap the garlic heads tightly in the foil. Place on a sheet pan and roast in the oven for 35 to 40 minutes. Check for doneness by piercing the heads with a skewer or paring knife. They are done when the center clove is soft. If the center clove is still firm, roast for another 5 minutes.

Once done, remove from the oven and let the heads cool at room temperature until they are cool enough to handle. Gently remove the cloves from their skin and spread out on a sheet pan, leaving space between the cloves. Place the pan in the freezer. Once frozen, transfer the cloves to a resealable plastic bag and store in the freezer. Thaw the garlic cloves as needed.

Alternatively, if using within 2 weeks, store the roasted garlic cloves, submerged in olive oil, in a clean, airtight container in the refrigerator.

compound butter: miso, anchovy, herb and lemon dill

MAKES ½ CUP (112 G) BUTTER

½ cup (112 g) unsalted butter (1 stick), at room temperature

Miso Butter
¼ cup (63 g) miso paste

Anchovy Butter
2 oz (55 g) anchovy fillets in oil, drained and minced

2 cloves garlic, grated, or 4 roasted cloves garlic

Herb Butter
4 cloves garlic, grated

1 tsp minced fresh rosemary

1 tsp minced fresh thyme

1 tsp minced fresh sage

½ tsp kosher salt

Lemon-Dill Butter
1 tbsp (4 g) minced fresh dill

2 cloves garlic, grated

Zest of 1 lemon

1 tsp fresh lemon juice

WHAT'S THAT INGREDIENT?

Miso paste is a Japanese seasoning made from fermented soybeans that are mixed with salt and koji, a mold used to make sake. The paste may also include barley, rice, rye or other grains. It can be found in plastic tubs or jars in the refrigerated section of Asian grocery stores, or next to refrigerated tofu in large grocery stores and natural food stores.

Here are some of my favorite compound butters that I like to have on hand. I have a compound butter for every occasion. If you are looking to add a little bit of salty umami to your dish, try a pat of miso butter or use it in the Sheet Pan Miso Butter–Rubbed Roast Chicken (page 38). Anchovy butter is great to add to a simple pasta dish, such as the Anchovy, Caper and Bread Crumb Pasta (page 25), or drizzled over boiled potatoes. Herb butter is my go-to butter over the Perfect Herb and Butter New York Strip (page 87) or roast chicken. Lemon dill butter can be used for the Slow-Roasted Lemon Butter Dill Salmon and Asparagus (page 100) or brushed over roast chicken breast.

In a bowl, combine the butter and your choice of seasonings. Using a hand mixer, whip until well combined.

Using a spatula, scrape the butter mixture out of the bowl and onto a sheet of parchment paper. Use the parchment paper to shape the butter into a log. Tightly wrap the butter with the parchment paper and twist the ends to seal. Refrigerate for 2 hours to allow the butter to set.

The compound butter will keep in the refrigerator for 1 week and in the freezer for 6 months.

*See image on page 160.

clarified butter, ghee and brown butter

1 lb (455 g) unsalted butter
(4 sticks), sliced

MAKES 1¹/₂ CUPS (337 G) BUTTER

You may have noticed that I used different types of cooked butter throughout this cookbook. That is because each butter has a distinct flavor. The main difference between these butters is the amount of time the milk solids of the butter cook. Clarified butter, which can be used in place of oil, cooks until the milk solids separate and they are then strained out. Ghee, used in the Crispy Za'atar Chicken and Cauliflower (page 41) and Roast Sweet Potatoes with Tahini Dressing (page 117), cooks longer, lightly browning the milks solids, which are then strained out, leaving the ghee with a light nutty flavor. Brown butter, used in the Creamy Brown Butter Tortellini (page 26) and Brown Butter Apple Tarte Tatin (page 152), cooks the longest, until the butter is golden brown. The browned milk solids are left in the butter, giving it an intense caramelized nutty flavor.

Place a fine-mesh strainer over a heatproof bowl. Line the strainer with cheesecloth and set aside.

In a saucepan, melt the butter over medium heat until the milk solids float to the top, about 1 minute. Then, follow the directions to complete your butter of choice.

Clarified Butter
Continue to simmer, adjusting the heat as needed to cook off the water until the milk solids begin to break up, about 2 minutes. When the butter just begins to foam, the water has cooked out of the butter.

Immediately pour the butter though the cheesecloth-lined strainer to remove the milk solids. Let the clarified butter cool at room temperature. Once the butter has cooled, transfer to an airtight container and refrigerate. Clarified butter will keep in the refrigerator for up to 6 months.

(continued)

clarified butter, ghee and brown butter (continued)

Ghee

Continue to simmer, adjusting the heat as needed to cook off the water until the milk solids begin to break up, about 2 minutes. When the butter begins to foam, the water has cooked out of the butter.

Continue to simmer until the foam just starts to develop a light brown color, about 1 minute. Keep an eye on it and stir occasionally to keep it from burning.

Pour the butter though the cheesecloth-lined strainer to remove the milk solids. Let the ghee cool at room temperature. Once the ghee has cooled, transfer to an airtight container and refrigerate. Ghee will keep in the refrigerator for up to 2 months.

Brown Butter

Continue to simmer, adjusting the heat as needed to cook off the water until the milk solids begin to break up, about 2 minutes. When the butter begins to foam, the water has cooked out of the butter.

Continue to simmer until the foam develops a deep amber color, 2 to 3 minutes. Keep an eye on it and stir occasionally to keep it from burning, as it can brown quickly.

Pour the brown butter into a heatproof bowl and let it cool at room temperature. Once the butter has cooled, stir and pour into ice cube molds. Chill in the refrigerator until the butter solidifies. Then, transfer the cubes to a resealable plastic bag. Brown butter will keep in the refrigerator for up to 2 weeks or in the freezer for 6 months.

acknowledgments

To my husband, Obed, you are my best friend, biggest fan and love of my life. I wouldn't trade our life together for anything. Thanks for always being there, making me laugh and having the patience to talk me off more than a few metaphorical ledges.

To Rebecca and Mary, for being my sounding board, the sources of countless laughs, endless encouragement and so much hand holding.

To "my girls", we joke often about my aversion to people, but you are my people. I am so blessed to call you friends. There is no one else I prefer to work, play, laugh, drink and eat with. Seriously.

To my family, thank you for loving me unconditionally and always being supportive. I am fully aware I can be a handful.

To Chef Herrmann and Chef Poe, who took the time to teach me and provide me with the tools and confidence I needed to take on my first cookbook.

To my fellow bloggers, you all inspire me every day. This is a weird and amazing job we get to do. How lucky are we?

To my local friends, thanks for encouraging me, being excited for me and checking in on me and dragging me out when I needed a break from work.

To my readers, without you I wouldn't have this amazing job and I would just be a weirdo screaming into the abyss of the Internet. I am amazed and inspired by you all!

To my pups Buster, Honey and Hank, I know you have no clue I am writing this, but you all have provided me with endless companionship, laughs and love. Also, thank you for cleaning up the kitchen floor every day.

To the Page Street team, thank you for this opportunity. It's been a blast and dream come true.

about the author

Meseidy Rivera is the creator, cook and photographer of the blog The Noshery, where you will find recipes that are always from scratch, ideas inspired by her travels and cooking techniques she learned along her journey from home cook to chef. Her recipes have been featured in *Saveur, Country Living,* BuzzFeed, The Kitchn, *Tasty Kitchen, The Pioneer Woman,* the Cooking Channel and the *New York Times.* She is also a regular contributor on The Pioneer Woman: Food and Friends.

A graduate of Platt College Culinary Institute, she has worked as a culinary assistant to Ree Drummond, The Pioneer Woman; and in event and television production catering and freelance recipe development. As a food blogger, photographer, food stylist and freelance recipe developer, she has also worked with and developed recipes for such brands as Pompeian, Tabasco, National Pork Board and Albertsons. Her dishes are influenced by her life as a former military brat, restaurant experience and Puerto Rican roots. She focuses on pairing exciting ingredients together and is always on a mission to create the perfect bite for you to re-create at home.

Meseidy lives in Chattanooga, Tennessee, with her husband, Obed, and three dogs Honey, Buster and Hank.

index

A

All the Herbs Roast Chicken Breast, 57

Anchovy, Caper and Bread Crumb Pasta, 25

Anchovy Butter, 178

Anchovy Butter Whipped Potatoes, Instant Pot, 125

Angostura bitters, in Orange and Whiskey–Glazed Chicken Thighs with Roast Cherries, 58

Apple Tarte Tatin, Brown Butter, 152

Apricots and Dates, Instant Pot Braised Lamb with, 76

Arugula and Watercress Salad, White Cheddar Dutch Baby with, 22

Asparagus, Slow-Roasted Lemon Butter Dill Salmon and, 100

Asparagus Salad, White Bean and, 137

B

bacon, in Bloody Mary Pepper Bacon–Wrapped Chicken, 46

bananas, in Sweet Plantain and Coconut Whipped Cream Crepes with Dulce de Leche, 143

Banh Mi, Chicken and Pâté, 42

Basil Pesto, My Favorite, 174

Bean and Asparagus Salad, White, 137

Beans and Pancetta, Cannellini, 129

beef

    Crispy Rosemary and Beef Tallow Potatoes, 121

    Instant Pot Beef Bourguignon, 80

    Instant Pot Classic Bolognese, 79

    Perfect Herb and Butter New York Strip, 87

    Skirt Steak with Orange and Shallot Gremolata, 84

    Slow Cooker Mulled Wine Short Ribs, 65–67

Blackberry and Peach Ginger Clafoutis, 156

Blackberry Sauce, Herb Pork Chops with, 71

Bloody Mary Pepper Bacon–Wrapped Chicken, 46

bok choy, in Sheet Pan Miso Butter–Rubbed Roast Chicken, 38

Bolognese, Instant Pot Classic, 79

Bone Broth, Instant Pot Roasted, 162

Bourguignon, Instant Pot Beef, 80

Bread Pudding with Vanilla Sauce, Tahini, 147

Broccoli with Lemony Yogurt, Crispy, 126

broth, in Instant Pot Roasted Bone Broth, 162

Brown Butter Apple Tarte Tatin, 152

Brown Butter Tortellini, Creamy, 26

Brussels Sprouts with Jalapeño Honey, Crispy Roasted, 114

Budino with Strawberry-Rhubarb Compote, Polenta, 144

butters

    Anchovy Butter, 178

    Brown Butter, 179–181

    Clarified Butter, 179

    Compound Butter: Miso, Anchovy, Herb and Lemon Dill, 178

    Ghee, 179–181

    Herb Butter, 178

    Lemon-Dill Butter, 178

    Miso Butter, 178

C

Cake, Lavender and Meyer Lemon Pound, 159

Cake, Upside-Down Peach-Ricotta Microwave, 151

Cannellini Beans and Pancetta, 129

capers, in Anchovy, Caper and Bread Crumb Pasta, 25

carrots, in Roast Carrots with Gochujang Glaze, 118

Cauliflower, Crispy Za'atar Chicken and, 41

Chamoy, Smoked Salmon Tostadas with, 103

Charcuterie Board, The Perfect, 88

Charred Zucchini with Pesto, 134

cheese

    Fontina Cheese Waffles with Cremini Mushroom Sauce, 18

Goat Cheese–Stuffed Shells with Honey and Chorizo, 14

Peach and Burrata Farro Salad, 29

The Perfect Charcuterie Board, 88

Red Wine–Poached Figs with Whipped Mascarpone, 148

Upside-Down Peach-Ricotta Microwave Cake, 151

Whipped Ricotta and Sardine Toast, 95

White Cheddar Dutch Baby with Arugula and Watercress Salad, 22

cherries, in Orange and Whiskey–Glazed Chicken Thighs with Roast Cherries, 58

Cherry and Dark Chocolate Galette, 140

chicken

    All the Herbs Roast Chicken Breast, 57

    Bloody Mary Pepper Bacon–Wrapped Chicken, 46

    Chicken and Pâté Banh Mi, 42

    Crispy Za'atar Chicken and Cauliflower, 41

    Ginger Chicken Meatball Ramen, 45

    Grapefruit and Pink Peppercorn Cream Chicken Thighs, 54

    Instant Pot Piri Piri Chicken Wings, 49

    Orange and Whiskey–Glazed Chicken Thighs with Roast Cherries, 58

Ras el Hanout Chicken with Prune and Olive Tapenade, 50

Sheet Pan Miso Butter–Rubbed Roast Chicken, 38

White Wine–Poached Chicken with Lemon Butter Sauce, 53

Chimichurri, 173

Chimichurri Red Snapper, Whole Roasted, 92

chocolate

    Cherry and Dark Chocolate Galette, 140

    Mexican Hot Chocolate Pots de Crème, 155

Chorizo, Goat Cheese–Stuffed Shells with Honey and, 14

chorizo, in Saffron Tortilla Española with Spanish Chorizo, 33

Clafoutis, Blackberry and Peach Ginger, 156

Clarified Butter, Ghee and Brown Butter, 179–181

coconut milk, in Shrimp and Coconut Green Curry, 96

Coconut Whipped Cream Crepes with Dulce de Leche, Sweet Plantain and, 143

Compote, Polenta Budino with Strawberry-Rhubarb, 144

Compound Butter: Miso, Anchovy, Herb and Lemon Dill, 178

couscous, in Herb Lamb Chops with Roast Eggplant Israeli Couscous Salad, 62–64

Crab and Chile Mango Lettuce Wraps, 108

Creamy Brown Butter Tortellini, 26

Creamy Polenta with Tomatoes and Baked Eggs, 21

Crepes with Dulce de Leche, Sweet Plantain and Coconut Whipped Cream, 143

Crispy Broccoli with Lemony Yogurt, 126

Crispy Roasted Brussels Sprouts with Jalapeño Honey, 114

Crispy Rosemary and Beef Tallow Potatoes, 121

Crispy Za'atar Chicken and Cauliflower, 41

Cured Egg Yolks, 169

Curry, Shrimp and Coconut Green, 96

D

Dates, Instant Pot Braised Lamb with Apricots and, 76

dill, in Slow-Roasted Lemon Butter Dill Salmon and Asparagus, 100

Dill Butter, 178

Dulce de Leche, Sweet Plantain and Coconut Whipped Cream Crepes with, 143

E

Edamame Succotash, 133

eggplant, in Herb Lamb Chops with Roast Eggplant Israeli Couscous Salad, 62–64

eggs

    Creamy Polenta with Tomatoes and Baked Eggs, 21

    Cured Egg Yolks, 169

    Saffron Tortilla Española with Spanish Chorizo, 33

F

Farro Salad, Peach and Burrata, 29

fennel, Mussels with Orange, Fennel and Black Olives, 99

Figs with Whipped Mascarpone, Red Wine–Poached, 148

fish

    Slow-Roasted Lemon Butter Dill Salmon and Asparagus, 100

    Smoked Trout and Rye Panzanella, 107

    Whipped Ricotta and Sardine Toast, 95

    Whole Roasted Chimichurri Red Snapper, 92

Five-Spice Pork, Slow Cooker Crispy, 83

Fontina Cheese Waffles with Cremini Mushroom Sauce, 18

G

Galette, Cherry and Dark Chocolate, 140

Garlic, Whole Roasted, 177

ginger, in Blackberry and Peach Ginger Clafoutis, 156

Ginger Chicken Meatball Ramen, 45

Goat Cheese–Stuffed Shells with Honey and Chorizo, 14

Gochujang Glaze, Roast Carrots with, 118

Grapefruit and Pink Peppercorn Cream Chicken Thighs, 54

gremolata, in Skirt Steak with Orange and Shallot Gremolata, 84

Guava and Pineapple Shrimp, 111

H

Harissa-Spiced Yogurt Dipping Sauce, Spiced Lamb Meatballs and, 72

Herb Butter, 178

Herb Lamb Chops with Roast Eggplant Israeli Couscous Salad, 62–64

Herb Pork Chops with Blackberry Sauce, 71

honey, in Crispy Roasted Brussels Sprouts with Jalapeño Honey, 114

I

Instant Pot Anchovy Butter Whipped Potatoes, 125

Instant Pot Beef Bourguignon, 80

Instant Pot Braised Lamb with Apricots and Dates, 76

Instant Pot Classic Bolognese, 79

Instant Pot Piri Piri Chicken Wings, 49

Instant Pot Risotto à la Carbonara, 17

Instant Pot Roasted Bone Broth, 162

J

Jalapeño Honey, Crispy Roasted Brussels Sprouts with, 114

Japanese Fried Rice, 30

L

lamb

    Herb Lamb Chops with Roast Eggplant Israeli Couscous Salad, 62–64

    Instant Pot Braised Lamb with Apricots and Dates, 76

    Spiced Lamb Meatballs and Harissa-Spiced Yogurt Dipping Sauce, 72

Lavender and Meyer Lemon Pound Cake, 159

lemons

    Crispy Broccoli with Lemony Yogurt, 126

    Lavender and Meyer Lemon Pound Cake, 159

    Lemon-Dill Butter, 178

    Peach and Burrata Farro Salad, 29

    Preserved Lemons, 166

    Ras el Hanout Chicken with Prune and Olive Tapenade, 50

    Slow-Roasted Lemon Butter Dill Salmon and Asparagus, 100

    White Wine–Poached Chicken with Lemon Butter Sauce, 53

Lettuce Wraps, Crab and Chile Mango, 108

M

Mango-Herb Salsa, Vadouvan Shrimp with, 104

Mascarpone, Red Wine–Poached Figs with Whipped, 148

Meatball Ramen, Ginger Chicken, 45

Meatballs and Harissa-Spiced Yogurt Dipping Sauce, Spiced Lamb, 72

Mediterranean Tomato Salad with Za'atar Pita Chips, 122

Mexican Hot Chocolate Pots de Crème, 155

Microwave Cake, Upside-Down Peach-Ricotta, 151

Miso Butter, 178

Miso Butter–Rubbed Roast Chicken, Sheet Pan, 38

Mole Pork Tacos, 75

mushrooms, in Fontina Cheese Waffles with Cremini Mushroom Sauce, 18

Mussels with Orange, Fennel and Black Olives, 99

My Favorite Basil Pesto, 174

N

nori, in Japanese Fried Rice, 30

O

Olive Tapenade, Ras el Hanout Chicken with Prune and, 50

Orange, Fennel and Black Olives, Mussels with, 99

Orange and Shallot Gremolata, Skirt Steak with, 84

Orange and Whiskey–Glazed Chicken Thighs with Roast Cherries, 58

P

pancakes, in White Cheddar Dutch Baby with Arugula and Watercress Salad, 22

Pancetta, Cannellini Beans and, 129

pancetta, in Instant Pot Risotto à la Carbonara, 17

Panzanella, Smoked Trout and Rye, 107

parsley, in Chimichurri, 173

pasta

Anchovy, Caper and Bread Crumb Pasta, 25

Creamy Brown Butter Tortellini, 26

Goat Cheese–Stuffed Shells with Honey and Chorizo, 14

Spicy Asian Noodle and Herb Salad, 34

pâté, in Slow Cooker Pork Rillettes (Rustic Pâté), 165

Pâté Banh Mi, Chicken and, 42

peaches

Blackberry and Peach Ginger Clafoutis, 156

Peach and Burrata Farro Salad, 29

Upside-Down Peach-Ricotta Microwave Cake, 151

peppercorns, in Grapefruit and Pink Peppercorn Cream Chicken Thighs, 54

Perfect Charcuterie Board, The, 88

Perfect Herb and Butter New York Strip, 87

Pesto, Charred Zucchini with, 134

Pesto, My Favorite Basil, 174

pickled vegetables, 42

Quick-Pickled Veggies, 170

pine nuts

Charred Zucchini with Pesto, 134

My Favorite Basil Pesto, 174

Pineapple Shrimp, Guava and, 111

Piri Piri Chicken Wings, Instant Pot, 49

pita bread, in Mediterranean Tomato Salad with Za'atar Pita Chips, 122

Plantain and Coconut Whipped Cream Crepes with Dulce de Leche, Sweet, 143

Polenta Budino with Strawberry-Rhubarb Compote, 144

Polenta with Tomatoes and Baked Eggs, Creamy, 21

pork

Herb Pork Chops with Blackberry Sauce, 71

Mole Pork Tacos, 75

Slow Cooker Crispy Five-Spice Pork, 83

Slow Cooker Pork Rillettes (Rustic Pâté), 165

Slow Cooker Tamarind Sticky Ribs, 68

potatoes

Crispy Rosemary and Beef Tallow Potatoes, 121

Instant Pot Anchovy Butter Whipped Potatoes, 125

Potato Salad with Fresh Herb Vinaigrette, 130

Saffron Tortilla Española with Spanish Chorizo, 33

Pound Cake, Lavender and Meyer Lemon, 159

Preserved Lemons, 166

prosciutto, in The Perfect Charcuterie Board, 88

Prune and Olive Tapenade, Ras el Hanout Chicken with, 50

Pudding with Vanilla Sauce, Tahini Bread, 147

Q

Quick-Pickled Veggies, 170

R

Ramen, Ginger Chicken Meatball, 45

Ras el Hanout Chicken with Prune and Olive Tapenade, 50

Red Snapper, Whole Roasted Chimichurri, 92

Red Wine–Poached Figs with Whipped Mascarpone, 148

rhubarb, in Polenta Budino with Strawberry-Rhubarb Compote, 144

rice, in Instant Pot Risotto à la Carbonara, 17

Rice, Japanese Fried, 30

ricotta, in Upside-Down Peach-Ricotta Microwave Cake, 151

Rillettes, Slow Cooker Pork, (Rustic Pâté), 165

Risotto à la Carbonara, Instant Pot, 17

Roast Carrots with Gochujang Glaze, 118

Roast Sweet Potatoes with Tahini Dressing, 117

Rosemary and Beef Tallow Potatoes, Crispy, 121

Rye Panzanella, Smoked Trout and, 107

S

Saffron Tortilla Española with Spanish Chorizo, 33

salads

Crab and Chile Mango Lettuce Wraps, 108

Edamame Succotash, 133

Herb Lamb Chops with Roast Eggplant Israeli Couscous Salad, 62–64

Mediterranean Tomato Salad with Za'atar Pita Chips, 122

Peach and Burrata Farro Salad, 29

Potato Salad with Fresh Herb Vinaigrette, 130

Smoked Trout and Rye Panzanella, 107

Spicy Asian Noodle and Herb Salad, 34

White Bean and Asparagus Salad, 137

White Cheddar Dutch Baby with Arugula and Watercress Salad, 22

Salmon and Asparagus, Slow-Roasted Lemon Butter Dill, 100

Salmon Tostadas with Chamoy, Smoked, 103

Sardine Toast, Whipped Ricotta and, 95

sausage

Goat Cheese–Stuffed Shells with Honey and Chorizo, 14

The Perfect Charcuterie Board, 88

Saffron Tortilla Española with Spanish Chorizo, 33

seafood

Crab and Chile Mango Lettuce Wraps, 108

Guava and Pineapple Shrimp, 111

Mussels with Orange, Fennel and Black Olives, 99

Shrimp and Coconut Green Curry, 96

Slow-Roasted Lemon Butter Dill Salmon and Asparagus, 100

Smoked Trout and Rye Panzanella, 107

Vadouvan Shrimp with Mango-Herb Salsa, 104

Whipped Ricotta and Sardine Toast, 95

Whole Roasted Chimichurri Red Snapper, 92

Shallot Gremolata, Skirt Steak with Orange and, 84

Sheet Pan Miso Butter–Rubbed Roast Chicken, 38

shrimp

Guava and Pineapple Shrimp, 111

Shrimp and Coconut Green Curry, 96

Vadouvan Shrimp with Mango-Herb Salsa, 104

Skirt Steak with Orange and Shallot Gremolata, 84

skyr, in Slow-Roasted Lemon Butter Dill Salmon and Asparagus, 100

Slow Cooker Crispy Five-Spice Pork, 83

Slow Cooker Mulled Wine Short Ribs, 65–67

Slow Cooker Pork Rillettes (Rustic Pâté), 165

Slow Cooker Tamarind Sticky Ribs, 68

Slow-Roasted Lemon Butter Dill Salmon and Asparagus, 100

Smoked Salmon Tostadas with Chamoy, 103

Smoked Trout and Rye Panzanella, 107

Spiced Lamb Meatballs and Harissa-Spiced Yogurt Dipping Sauce, 72

Spicy Asian Noodle and Herb Salad, 34

steaks

    Perfect Herb and Butter New York Strip, 87

    Skirt Steak with Orange and Shallot Gremolata, 84

Sticky Ribs, Slow Cooker Tamarind, 68

Strawberry-Rhubarb Compote, Polenta Budino with, 144

Succotash, Edamame, 133

Sweet Plantain and Coconut Whipped Cream Crepes with Dulce de Leche, 143

Sweet Potatoes with Tahini Dressing, Roast, 117

T

Tacos, Mole Pork, 75

Tahini Bread Pudding with Vanilla Sauce, 147

Tahini Dressing, Roast Sweet Potatoes with, 117

tallow, in Crispy Rosemary and Beef Tallow Potatoes, 121

Tamarind Sticky Ribs, Slow Cooker, 68

Tapenade, Ras el Hanout Chicken with Prune and Olive, 50

Tarte Tatin, Brown Butter Apple, 152

Tomato Salad with Za'atar Pita Chips, Mediterranean, 122

Tomatoes and Baked Eggs, Creamy Polenta with, 21

Tortellini, Creamy Brown Butter, 26

Tortilla Española with Spanish Chorizo, Saffron, 33

Tostadas with Chamoy, Smoked Salmon, 103

Trout and Rye Panzanella, Smoked, 107

U

Upside-Down Peach-Ricotta Microwave Cake, 151

V

Vadouvan Shrimp with Mango-Herb Salsa, 104

Vanilla Sauce, Tahini Bread Pudding with, 147

W

Waffles with Cremini Mushroom Sauce, Fontina Cheese, 18

Watercress Salad, White Cheddar Dutch Baby with Arugula and, 22

Whipped Ricotta and Sardine Toast, 95

Whiskey-Glazed Chicken Thighs with Roast Cherries, Orange and, 58

White Bean and Asparagus Salad, 137

White Cheddar Dutch Baby with Arugula and Watercress Salad, 22

White Wine–Poached Chicken with Lemon Butter Sauce, 53

Whole Roasted Chimichurri Red Snapper, 92

Whole Roasted Garlic, 177

wine

    Red Wine–Poached Figs with Whipped Mascarpone, 148

    Slow Cooker Mulled Wine Short Ribs, 65–67

    White Wine–Poached Chicken with Lemon Butter Sauce, 53

Wraps, Crab and Chile Mango Lettuce, 108

Y

Yogurt, Crispy Broccoli with Lemony, 126

Yogurt Dipping Sauce, Spiced Lamb Meatballs and Harissa-Spiced, 72

Z

Za'atar Chicken and Cauliflower, Crispy, 41

Za'atar Pita Chips, Mediterranean Tomato Salad with, 122

Zucchini with Pesto, Charred, 134